HOUSES
MAISONS
HÄUSER

HOUSES
MAISONS
HÄUSER

h.f.ullmann

Idea and Concept/Idée et conception/Idee und Konzept: **Paco Asensio, Hugo Kliczkowski**

Editor and Texts/Coordination éditoriale et rédaction/Verlagskoordination und Text: **Alejandro Bahamón**

Introduction/Introduction/Einleitung: **Hugo Kliczkowski**

Art Direction/Direction artistique/Art Direktor: **Mireia Casanovas Soley**

Layout/Maquette/Grafik Design: **Ignasi Gracia Blanco, Cris Tarradas**

English translation/Traduction en anglais/Übersetzung ins Englische: **Michael Brunelle, Beatriz Cortabarria**

French translation/Traduction en français/Übersetzung ins Französische: **Arnaud Dupin de Beyssat**

German translation/Traduction en allemand/Übersetzung ins Deutsche: **Susanne Engler**

Cover design/Design de la jaquette/Coverdesign: Simone Sticker

Editorial project/Projet éditorial/Verlagsprojekt:

© **LOFT Publications**
Via Laietana 32, 4° Of. 92
08003 Barcelona. Spain
Tel.: +34 932 688 088
Fax: +34 932 687 073
loft@loftpublications.com
www.loftpublications.com

Original title: HOUSES - CASAS - HÄUSER
ISBN: 978-3-8331-1588-2

© 2008 Tandem Verlag GmbH
h.f.ullmann is an imprint of Tandem Verlag GmbH
Special edition
ISBN: 978-3-8331-4899-6

Printed in China

10 9 8 7 6 5 4 3 2 1
X IX VIII VII VI V IV III II I

www.ullmann-publishing.com

Summary

Sommaire

Inhalt

© Arriet Denis

"I eagerly search for houses that are 'houses for people' and not houses for architects. It is an important quest. One can say that a house for people emanates love. Allow me to explain this from a filmmaker's point of view; imagine being in a restaurant, not one of those fancy restaurants where the arbitrary intervention of the waiters and the sommeliers destroy my poem, but one of those quaint, small cafés where two or three patrons have just finished drinking their coffees and are chatting.

The plates, glasses, bottles, the salt, the pepper, the napkins, napkin holder... are all still on the table. Observe the total disarray in the relationships between these objects; they have served their purpose, they have all been handled by one guest or another. The distances that separate them represent the measure of daily life. It is a mathematically coherent composition; there is no wrong place in the choice of placement, no hiatus, no false intentions. If a film director who was not contaminated by Hollywood were there at that moment, filming a close up of that still life it would be a testament to pure harmony. Could this be possible? Yes, and how unfortunate are those who seek the false, pretentious, commercial, and academic harmony of Vignola circa 1925, or of the latest fad.

Le Corbusier, in his 1929 American prologue for Precisions

« Je cherche ardemment des maisons qui soient des 'maisons pour les gens' et non des maisons pour architectes. C'est une quête importante. On peut dire qu'il émane de l'amour d'une maison pour les gens. Permettez-moi d'expliquer cela du point de vue d'un réalisateur de cinéma : imaginez que vous êtes dans un restaurant, pas un de ces restaurants de luxe où l'intervention arbitraire des garçons et du sommelier détruit mon poème, mais dans un de ces pittoresques petits cafés où deux ou trois clients finissent de boire leur café en discutant.

Les assiettes, les verres, les bouteilles, le sel, le poivre, la nappe, les pinces à nappes... tout est encore sur la table. Remarquez la totale confusion dans les relations entre ces objets ; ils ont rempli leur fonction, ils ont été manipulés par un ou l'autre des convives. Les distances qui les séparent représentent la mesure de la vie quotidienne. C'est une composition mathématiquement cohérente ; il n'y a pas de mauvais emplacement dans cette disposition, pas de hiatus, pas de fausse intention. Si un réalisateur qui n'est pas contaminé par Hollywood se trouvait là à ce moment, et filmait en plan rapproché cette nature morte, ce serait un testament à l'harmonie pure. Cela est-il possible ? Oui, et combien malheureux sont ceux qui recherchent cette harmonie fausse, prétentieuse, commerciale et académique de Vignola vers 1925, ou celle de la toute dernière mode. »

Précisions sur un état présent de l'architecture et de l'urbanisme, Le Corbusier, préface de l'édition américaine de 1929

„Ich suche mit großem Eifer nach den Häusern, die „Häuser von Menschen", und nicht Häuser von Architekten sind. Das ist eine wirklich ernste Angelegenheit. Man kann sagen, dass ein Haus von Menschen Liebe ist. Lasst mich deshalb ein Beispiel aus dem Kino anführen. Beobachten Sie einen Tagen, aber nicht in einem dieser Luxusrestaurants, in denen das eigenmächtige Eingreifen der Kellner und der „Sommeliers" mein Gedicht zerstört, sondern eine kleine, beliebte Kneipe, in der zwei oder drei Tischgäste gerade ihren Kaffee beendet haben und sich noch ein wenig unterhalten.

Der Tisch ist noch voller Gläser, Flaschen, Teller, die Ölflasche, das Salz, der Pfeffer, die Servietten, der Serviettenhalter, usw. Betrachten Sie die unausweichliche Ordnung, die alle diese Objekte untereinander haben; alle haben zu etwas gedient, alle wurden von der Hand des einen oder anderen Tischgastes aufgenommen, die Abstände, die zwischen ihnen existieren, sind aus dem Leben gegriffene Maße. Es handelt sich um eine mathematisch angeordnete Komposition, es gibt keinen falschen Platz, keinen Hiatus, keine Täuschung. Falls sich ein Cineast, der nicht von Hollywood geblendet ist, hier befände und dieses Stillleben „im Vordergrund" filmen würde, hätten wir ein Zeugnis der reinen Harmonie. Ist das möglich? Ja, und unglücklich sind die, die nach den falschen Harmonien suchen, den vorgetäuschten, kommerziellen, akademischen Harmonien von Vignola im Jahr 1925 oder der letzten Mode".

Le Corbusier, im Amerikanischen Prolog 1929, Precisiones

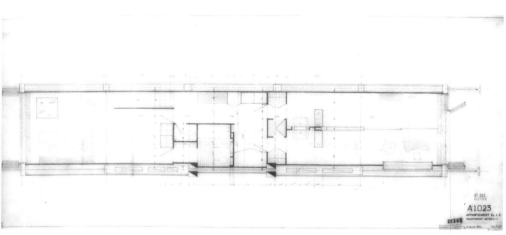

Books, Houses, Cities, and Architects

Why this book?
Because we like to look at houses and design plans, and we love to edit them. A desire (not always possible) is to attract the interest of the reader. We must confess that after so many years in the publishing profession, we truly do not know how to achieve that. We have some ideas and some convictions as well, and we rely on them. We do not know and we do not expect to find out when and why a person chooses a book and, by chance, decides to take it home. We could imagine that it is to share some dream. And that dream, in this case, is a house, a plan, a living space.

And we ask ourselves:
Is an empty house inviting enough to justify this? Does a space that is not our own stimulate our desire to learn more about it? Can a house, wherever it may be, serve as an inspiration and as a model for a similar one?
Is its cost, even if it does not fit our budget, an obstacle for desiring it, or do we want it precisely because it is unattainable?

Desires, fantasies, ambitions, status symbol or not, houses are central to our dreams, and fundamentally, a basic necessity.

Livres, maisons, villes, et architectes

Pourquoi ce livre ?
Parce que nous aimons regarder les maisons et leurs plans de conception, et que nous aimons les publier. Un désir (pas toujours possible) d'attirer l'intérêt du lecteur. Nous devons avouer qu'après tant d'années dans l'édition nous ne savons toujours pas comment y parvenir. Nous nous appuyons sur quelques idées, et aussi sur quelques convictions. Nous ne savons pas, et nous ne pensons pas le découvrir un jour, pourquoi quelqu'un choisit un livre et décide, par hasard, de l'emmener chez lui. Nous pouvons imaginer que c'est pour partager quelque rêve. Et que ce rêve, ici, est une maison, un plan, un espace de vie.

Et nous nous demandons :
Une maison vide est-elle suffisamment accueillante pour justifier ce geste ? Un espace qui n'est pas le nôtre peut-il à ce point stimuler notre désir d'en savoir plus ? Une maison, quelle qu'elle soit, peut-elle inspirer ou servir de modèle à une autre similaire ? Son prix, même s'il ne correspond pas à notre budget, est-il un obstacle pour la désirer, ou la voulons-nous précisément parce qu'elle est inaccessible ?

Désirs, fantaisies, ambitions, symbole social ou non, les maisons sont au centre de nos rêves, et demeurent, fondamentalement, une nécessité vitale pour nous.

Bücher, Häuser, Städte und Architekten

Warum dieses Buch?
Da wir uns gerne Häuser und Pläne anschauen, und sie leidenschaftlich gerne veröffentlichen. Unser Wunsch ist es (was nicht immer möglich ist), auch das Interesse der Leser damit zu wecken. Wir müssen aber zugeben, dass wir nach so vielen Jahren in der Verlagswelt eigentlich immer noch nicht wissen, wie man das macht. Wir haben da ein paar Ideen und auch einige Gewissheiten, und auf diese setzen wir. Wir wissen nicht und können nicht wissen, wann und warum ein Leser ein Buch auswählt und es, ganz zufällig, nach Hause mitnimmt. Wir könnten denken, dass vielleicht Träume darin verwickelt sind. Und diese Träume sind in diesem Fall ein Haus, ein Projekt, ein Raum zum Wohnen.
Und wir stellen uns ein paar Fragen:
Ein Haus, in dem wir nicht wohnen, lädt es uns zum darin Wohnen ein? Eine Umgebung, die nicht unsere ist, würden wir sie gerne kennen lernen?
Ein Haus, egal, wo es sich befindet, ist es für uns ein interessantes Modell für andere, ähnliche Häuser? Wenn die Kosten nicht unseren Möglichkeiten entsprechen, ist es ein Hindernis, um es uns zu wünschen, oder wollen wir es im Gegenteil, weil es unerreichbar ist?
Wünsche, Phantasien, Ambitionen, Illusionen, Symbol für die gesellschaftliche Stellung oder nicht, Häuser bilden einen Teil unserer Träume, und vor allen Dingen sind sie lebensnotwendig.

Houses, Cities, and Architects

House, can, casa, maison, logis, home, haus, shack, vohnung, building, apartment, loft, penthouse, duplex, residence, etcetera.

Yet another question: is a house a building to live in? "A house is a home", Le Corbusier used to proclaim. He also proposed the idea that a house can be a machine to live in.

A house can be so many other things as well, since it constitutes the unit that, together with other elements, shapes and gives meaning to the urban environment, to the city.

And it is the latter that shapes the character of a house, therefore we ask, do the two interact?

Andrea Palladio (1508-1580) wrote in chapter twelve of his Book II that "a city is nothing more than a large house, and on the other hand, a house is nothing more than a small city."

We live in and inhabit houses, we dream about them, we imagine them, and we think about them as described by the great master Frank Lloyd Wright (1869-1959).

"Thinking is dealing with simplicity, and that means thinking of the whole as a single vision..." And he added in referring to the project, that drawing "five lines where three are sufficient is simply foolish."

But what do those houses look like? Are they like the others? And which others? Different, personal, we know that often they are more than a reflection of our needs. Luckily.

Maisons, villes et architectes

Maison, house, casa, haus, logis, bâtiment, appartement, loft, penthouse, duplex, résidence, etc.

Et encore une autre question : la maison est-elle un édifice où habiter ? « Une maison est un foyer », disait Le Corbusier, en ajoutant qu'une maison pouvait être aussi une machine à habiter.

Une maison peut également représenter d'autres choses, car elle constitue l'unité qui, avec d'autres éléments, crée et donne du sens à l'environnement urbain, à la ville.

Et comme c'est cette dernière qui forme le caractère d'une maison, nous nous demandons alors si les deux interfèrent.

Andrea Palladio (1508-1580) écrivait, au chapitre 12 de son Livre II que « une ville n'est rien d'autre qu'une grande maison, et d'un autre côté, une maison n'est autre qu'une petite ville ».

Nous occupons et habitons dans des maisons, nous en rêvons, nous les imaginons, et nous y pensons, soulignait le grand maître Frank Lloyd Wright (1869-1959). « Penser est négocier avec la simplicité, et cela signifie penser à l'ensemble avec une vision unique... » Et il ajoutait, en se référant au projet, que dessiner « cinq lignes lorsque trois suffisent est tout simplement idiot. »

Mais à quoi ressemblent ces maisons ? Sont-elles comme les autres ? Et quelles autres ? Différentes, personnelles, nous savons qu'elles sont souvent plus qu'un reflet de nos besoins. Heureusement.

Häuser, Städte und Architekten

Casa, can, house, maison, logis, home, Haus, choza, Wohnung, edificio, piso, loft, penthouse, duplex, vivienda, usw...

Noch mehr Fragen: Ist ein Haus ein Gebäude zum Wohnen?

„Ein Haus ist ein Heim", ließ uns Le Corbusier denken, und er warf gleichzeitig das Problem auf, dass ein Haus auch eine Wohnmaschine sein kann.

Es kann auch noch etwas anderes sein, da das Haus in einer Einheit entsteht, die zusammen mit anderen Elementen, die Stadt bildet, und ihr Sinn gibt.

Und es ist die Stadt, die dem Haus seinen Charakter verleiht. Gibt es eine Wechselbeziehung zwischen beiden?

Andrea Palladio (1508-1580) schrieb im 12. Kapitel seines 2. Buches „Die Stadt ist nichts anderes als ein großes Haus und, im Gegensatz dazu, das Haus ist eine kleine Stadt".

Wir leben und wohnen in Häusern, wir träumen, wir stellen sie uns vor und wir denken an sie in dem Sinne, den der Meister Frank Lloyd Wright (1869-1959) aufzeigte.

„Denken bedeutet, einen Pakt mit der Einfachheit abschließen, und das bedeutet mit einer einzigen Vision für das Gesamte zu denken..." Und er fügte hinzu, wobei er sich auf die Planung bezog, dass beim Zeichnen, „fünf Linien dort, wo drei ausreichen würden, dies einfach dumm ist".

There are people who wish to live in cities like Priene, conforming to the concepts of geometric regularity of Hipodamo de Mileto, in the transitional era between Classicism and Hellenism?

Or would they like living in houses like those in the Fachada Delta project (1954) or Barrio de Xul Solar (1953), (Óscar Agustín Alejandro Schulz Solari, 1887-1963).

Or prefer the houses in Paris where Juan Gris (José Victoriano González, 1887-1927) used to teach.

Or in the DOM-INO House (1916) by Le Corbusier (Charles Édouard Jeanneret-Gris, 1887-1965), or in his apartment buildings in Marseilles, Nantes-Rezé; Briey-en-Fôret; Berlin-Charlottenburg and Firminy-Vert, applying the laws of harmony of his modular.

Or living in Villa Mairea (1937) by Finnish architect Alvar Aalto (1898-1976).

A book, this book about houses, our houses, the houses that others live in, bordering what could be considered their own parameters, show examples, and perhaps prototypes.

We say prototypes because when we speak of houses we also refer to behaviors, to styles, and ultimately, to culture.

This is especially true if we look at them as lifestyles and customs, the knowledge of an era, a social group. A reader looks at the book and sees the houses: does he or she look at them and see them with the purpose of choosing one, or to learn, by inference, what other people have desired?

Il y a des gens qui souhaitent vivre dans des villes comme Priène, suivant le concept de tracé régulier géométrique d'Hippodamos de Milet, à l'époque de transition entre classicisme et hellénisme.

Ou dans des maisons comme celles du projet Fachada Delta (1954) ou du Barrio (1953) de Xul Solar (Oscar Agustin Alejandro Schulz Solari, 1887-1963).

Ou dans les maisons de Paris où Juan Gris (José Victoriano González, 1887-1927) enseignait.

Ou dans la maison DOM-INO (1916) de Le Corbusier (Charles-Édouard Jeanneret-Gris, 1887-1965), dans ses Cités radieuses de Marseille, Nantes-Rezé et Briey-en-Forêt, ou ses unités d'habitation de Berlin-Charlottenburg et Firminy-Vert, où il appliqué ses principes d'harmonie du modulor.

Ou dans la Villa Mairea (1937) de l'architecte finlandais Alvar Aalto (1898-1976).

Un livre, ce livre sur des maisons, nos maisons, des maisons où vivent les autres, s'approchant de ce qu'on peut considérer comme leurs propres paramètres, montre des exemples et probablement des prototypes.

Nous écrivons prototypes parce que lorsque nous parlons de maisons nous parlons également de comportements, de styles, et finalement, de culture.

Cela est particulièrement vrai si nous les considérons comme des styles et des habitudes de vie, la connaissance d'une époque, d'un groupe social. Un lecteur ouvre ce livre et voit des maisons : les regarde-t-il dans le but d'en choisir une, ou pour apprendre, par déduction, ce que d'autres ont désiré ?

Aber wie sind diese Häuser? Sind sie wie die anderen?

Und welche anderen? Anders, persönlich, wir wissen, dass sie oft mehr als die Widerspiegelung unserer Bedürfnisse sind. Zum Glück.

Es gibt Menschen, die in Städten wie Priene leben möchten, und die den Konzepten der geometrischen Regelmäßigkeit von Hippodamos von Milet folgen, in jenen Epochen des Übergangs von der Klassik zum Hellenismus.

Oder in Häusern wie die des Projektes Fachada Delta (1954) oder Barrio (1953) von Xul Solar (Óscar Agustín Alejandro Schulz Solari, 1887-1963).

Oder in den Häusern von Paris, die Juan Gris (José Victoriano González, 1887-1927) zeigte.

Oder in dem Haus DOM-INO (1916) von Le Corbusier (Charles Édouard Jeanneret-Gris, 1887-1965), oder in seinen Wohneinheiten in Marseille, Nantes-Rezé; Briey-en-Fôret; Berlin-Charlottenburg und Firminy-Vert, um sich von den harmonischen Gesetzen des Modularen hinreißen zu lassen.

Oder in der Villa Mairea (1937) des finnischen Architekten Alvar Aalto (1898-1976).

Ein Buch, unser Buch über Häuser, unsere Häuser, die Häuser, in denen andere wohnen, das sich dem annähert, was die Parameter selbst sein könnten, zeigt Beispiele, vielleicht Prototypen.

Prototypen, da wir, wenn wir über Häuser reden, auch über Verhaltensweisen, Stile, und letzten Endes über Kultur reden.

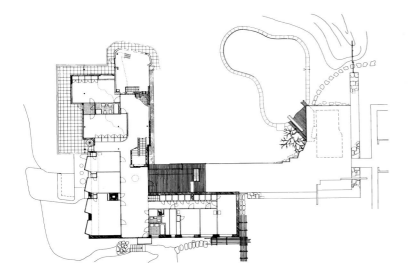

This way, step by step, project by project, house by house, we build a continuum, an understanding of the culture that allows us to learn which house is worth living in and which is not.
And by which architects?

Architects

Oscar Niemeyer (1907) already warned us that he "felt in his heart, that life is more important than architecture. Or that the type of architecture that he preferred was one where courage and freedom of form were essential."
Oscar Niemeyer, by Matthieu Salvaing (HK Publisher). And he had a point when he declared that, "beauty is something that a person is entitled to, because it improves everyone's quality of life."

Alvar Aalto stated at the Architectural Association (AA) conference of 1950 in London that "an architect is someone who manipulates materials and forms; what he says has no value, what he does is what counts."

Hans Hollein (1934) said that for him "architecture is not simply a solution to a given problem, but a kind of opinion."
Houses, we all know, are more than just buildings, they are icons, and as such we display them. Sometimes we show ourselves WITH them, and other times IN them.

De cette manière, étape par étape, projet par projet, maison par maison, nous construisons un continuum, une compréhension de la culture qui nous permet d'apprendre dans quelle maison on pourrait vivre.
Et grâce à quels architectes ?

Architectes

Oscar Niemeyer (1907) nous prévenait déjà qu'il « sentait dans son cœur que la vie est plus importante que l'architecture. Ou que le type d'architecture qu'il préférait était celui où le courage et la liberté de la forme étaient essentiels. »
Oscar Niemeyer, par Matthieu Salvaing (HK Publisher). Et il précisait que « la beauté est quelque chose auquel une personne a droit, parce qu'elle améliore la qualité de vie de chacun. »

En 1950, Alvar Aalto assurait à la conférence de l'Architectural Association (AA) à Londres que « un architecte est quelqu'un qui manipule des matières et des formes ; ce qu'il dit n'a pas de valeur, seul ce qu'il fait compte. »

Hans Hollein (1934) avouait que, pour lui, « l'architecture n'est pas simplement une solution à un problème donné, mais une forme d'opinion. »
Les maisons, nous le savons tous, sont plus que de simples bâtiments, ce sont des icônes, et nous les présentons en tant que telles. Parfois, nous nous montrons AVEC elles et, d'autres fois, EN elles.

Vor allem, wenn wir sie als ein Ganzes aus Lebensweisen und Gewohnheiten, den Kenntnissen einer Epoche oder einer sozialen Gruppe verstehen.
Ein Leser betrachtet das Buch, er sieht die Häuser. Betrachtet er sie so, als ob er eins aussuchen würde? Oder um zu wissen, um daraus abzuleiten, was andere Menschen sich wünschten?
So wird Schritt für Schritt, Projekt für Projekt, Haus für Haus ein Continuum aufgebaut, ein Wissen um die Kultur, die es uns erlaubt zu wissen, welches Haus es verdient, bewohnt zu werden, und welches nicht.
Und von welchen Architekten?

Architekten

Oscar Niemeyer (1907), sagte uns bereits, dass "es ihm bewusst sei, dass das Leben wichtiger als die Architektur sei. Oder dass die Art von Architektur, die er bevorzugte, die sei, in der der Mut und die gestalterische Freiheit grundlegend sind".
Oscar Niemeyer, von Matthieu Salvaing (Verlag HK). Und es machte auch Sinn, als er erklärte, dass „die Schönheit etwas sei, worauf der Mensch ein Recht hat, da sie das Leben der Menschen verbessert".

Alvar Aalto sagte 1950 auf einer Konferenz der Architectural Association (AA) in London, dass „ein Architekt jemand sei, der mit den Materialien und den Formen umgeht; was er sagt, ist nichts wert, das, was etwas wert ist, ist, was er tut".
Hans Hollein (1934) wies darauf hin, dass für ihn „die

As far back as 1919 Walter Gropius (1883-1969) had a vision, to which he assigned a technical name, Bauhaus (house under construction), because he believed that a house was "synonymous with a wealth of ideas, precision in its execution, and capability of adaptation."

A house is an interpretation of life and the surrounding environment, a human and created environment.

Gropius agreed with his peers that a house promotes reflection and the development of future society, when understood in more of an individual context than a social one.

We are what we build, what we live in.

When we look at the projects in this book we smile thinking about classical Greece where artists were famous and well respected, where their personal talents, not their social origins, gave them prestige. Unlike those times, the architects and artists of later Hellenistic period admitted that their function was more contemplative than practical. The purpose of their art and architecture was to represent reality, not to modify it.

And during the Roman period, the status of artists was even lower, the designer was mistaken for a contractor or an worker, a situation that lasted until the Middle Ages.

Dès 1919, Walter Gropius (1883-1969) eut une vision à laquelle il associa un nom technique, Bauhaus (maison de la construction), car il pensait qu'une maison était « synonyme de richesse des idées, de précision dans l'exécution, et de capacité d'adaptation. »

Une maison est une interprétation de la vie et de l'environnement, un environnement humain et créé.

Gropius ajoutait avec ses pairs qu'une maison favorise la réflexion et le développement de la société future lorsqu'elle est comprise dans un contexte plus individuel que social.

Nous sommes ce que nous bâtissons, ce qui nous abrite.

Lorsque nous étudions les projets présentés dans ce livre, nous sourions en pensant à la Grèce classique où des artistes furent célèbres et respectés, devant leur prestige à talent personnel, et non à leurs origines sociales. Contrairement à cette époque, les architectes et les artistes la période hellénistique ultérieure admirent que leur fonction était plus contemplative que pratique. L'objectif de leur art et de leur architecture était de représenter la réalité, et non pas de la modifier.

Au cours de la période romaine, le statut des artistes était encore moins enviable, les concepteurs étant considérés comme des maître d'oeuvre ou des ouvriers, une situation qui perdura jusqu'au Moyen Âge.

Comme cette confusion prévaut toujours, la même description serait encore valable aujourd'hui.

Architektur nicht nur einfach die Lösung eines gegebenen Problems ist, sondern so eine Art Meinung".

Häuser sind, wie wir bereits wissen, etwas mehr als Bauten, sie sind Ikonen, und so zeigen wir sie. Oft zeigen wir uns MIT ihnen, und andere Male zeigen wir uns IN ihnen.

Schon 1919 hatte Walter Gropius (1883-1969) eine Vision, der er einen programmatischen Namen gab, Bauhaus, da er der Ansicht war, dass Haus „gleichbedeutend mit Ideenreichtum, Genauigkeit der Ausführung und Anpassungsfähigkeit" sei.

Das Haus als Interpretation des Lebens und der Umwelt. Menschliche und bebaute Umwelt.

Gropius vereinbarte mit den Seinen, dass ein Haus einen Impuls zum Nachdenken und zur Entwicklung der Zukunft der Gesellschaft sei, das man eher sozial als individuell verstehen sollte.

Wir sind genauso das, was wir bauen, wie das, was wir bewohnen.

Wenn man also die Häuser in diesem Band sieht, lächeln wir bei dem Gedanken, dass im klassischen Griechenland die Künstler berühmte und respektierte Persönlichkeiten waren, und dass es ihr persönliches Talent und nicht ihre gesellschaftliche Herkunft war, das sie berühmt machte.

Im Gegensatz zu jener Zeit erkannten die Architekten und Künstler der späteren, hellenistischen Epoche an, dass ihre Funktion eher kontemplativ als praktisch sei, ihre Architektur und ihre Kunst dienten zur

Since this confusion still prevails, the same description would still be valid today.
And thinking about the future, how will it be, what will our books be like, our houses, our cities?

"...nothing that comes from the past can be reborn, but it will never disappear completely either..."

Alvar Aalto, Painters and Masons, Jousimies, 1921

Et penser à comment sera l'avenir, quel qu'il soit, à quoi ressembleront nos livres, nos maisons, nos villes ?

« ... rien de ce qui vient du passé ne peut être ressuscité, mais rien ne disparaîtra jamais non plus complètement... »

Alvar Aalto, Peintres et Maçons, Jousimies, 1921

Darstellung der Wirklichkeit, und nicht dazu, sie zu verändern.
Und in der Zeit der Römer war die gesellschaftliche Anerkennung der Künstler sogar noch geringer. Der Planer wird mit dem Erbauer oder dem Ausführenden verwechselt, diese Situation ändert sich bis zum Mittelalter nicht.

Da diese Verwechslung auch noch weiterhin besteht, könnte man heutzutage die gleiche Beschreibung geben.
Und denken: Wie wird es morgen sein? Wir werden unsere Bücher sein? Unsere Häuser? Unsere Städte?

„...nichts, was aus der Vergangenheit kommt, kann wieder geboren werden, aber es verschwindet auch nicht vollständig..."

Alvar Aalto, Painters and Masons, Jousimies, 1921

Hugo Alberto Kliczkowski Juritz

HOUSES

MAISONS / HÄUSER

This house is located in the Alto de Pinheiros area of the Brazilian city of São Paulo. According to the architect, São Paulo is possibly the least attractive city in the world, a large urban complex where chaos and disorder reign, and where the architecture is almost always unrelated to its setting. This project is no exception; it takes the form of a large white perimeter wall that wraps around the property, isolating it from its context and creating its own views facing the house. The clients are a couple working in the field of advertising, and early in the process they specified the things that should drive the design project. These included a very large shelf that would occupy the double-height living room, large-scale windows that open to the garden, a long swimming pool, a kitchen complete with an orange dining table in the center, two symmetrical marble stairways framed by natural light, a custom-designed studio; and sophisticated spaces with elegant proportions that are permanently linked with the exterior.

Gama-Issa House

Marcio Kogan

São Paulo, Brazil, 2001
Photos © Arnaldo Pappalardo

Cette maison est située dans le quartier Alto de Pinheiros de Sao Paolo (Brésil). Pour l'architecte, il s'agit probablement de la ville la moins belle du monde, un grand complexe urbain où règne le chaos et le désordre, et dans lequel il est rare qu'un projet architectural parvienne à établir quelque dialogue avec son environnement. Ce projet-ci ne fait pas exception en ce qu'il montre un vaste mur périphérique blanc qui isole

Dieses Haus befindet sich im Viertel Alto de Pinheiros in der brasilianischen Stadt São Paulo, die, wie der Architekt sagt, vielleicht die hässlichste Stadt der Welt ist. Eine riesige Stadt, in der Chaos und Unordnung herrschen und in der nur sehr selten die architektonische Planung im Dialog mit der Umgebung steht. Der Fall dieses Gebäudes ist somit keine Ausnahme. Es handelt sich um eine große, weiße Hülle in Form einer Mauer, die das Haus von seiner

la propriété du quartier et crée l'unique paysage visible depuis la maison. Les clients, un couple travaillant dans la publicité, ont défini dès le début les points forts du programme : une immense bibliothèque dans la salle de séjour, au plafond pleine hauteur ; de vastes baies ouvrant sur le jardin ; une piscine tout en longueur ; une cuisine aménagée avec une table orange au centre ; deux escaliers symétriques en marbre éclairés par la lumière naturelle ; un bureau sur mesure ; et, plus généralement, des espaces sophistiqués, de proportions élégantes, en relation permanente avec l'extérieur.

Umwelt isoliert. Innerhalb dieser Mauern wird eine eigene Landschaft geschaffen, die sich bis zum Haus erstreckt. Die Kunden, ein Paar, das im Werbesektor tätig ist, hatten schon von Anfang an sehr genaue Vorstellungen von dem, was sie sich für ihr Haus wünschten: Ein riesiges Regal, das sich über das gesamte Wohnzimmer mit einer Decke in doppelter Höhe erstreckt, große Fenster, die sich zum Garten hin öffnen, einen längs verlaufenden Swimmingpool, eine Küche, in deren Mitte ein orangener Esstisch stehen sollte, zwei symmetrisch verlaufende Marmortreppen, auf die Tageslicht fällt, ein auf Maß gearbeitetes Atelier und im allgemeinen edle Räume in eleganten Proportionen, die ständig mit außen in Verbindung stehen sollten.

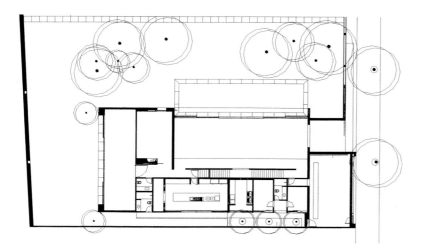

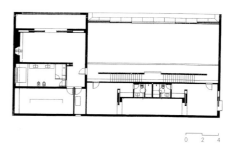

Ground floor
Rez-de-chaussée
Erdgeschoss

First floor
Premier étage
Erster Stock

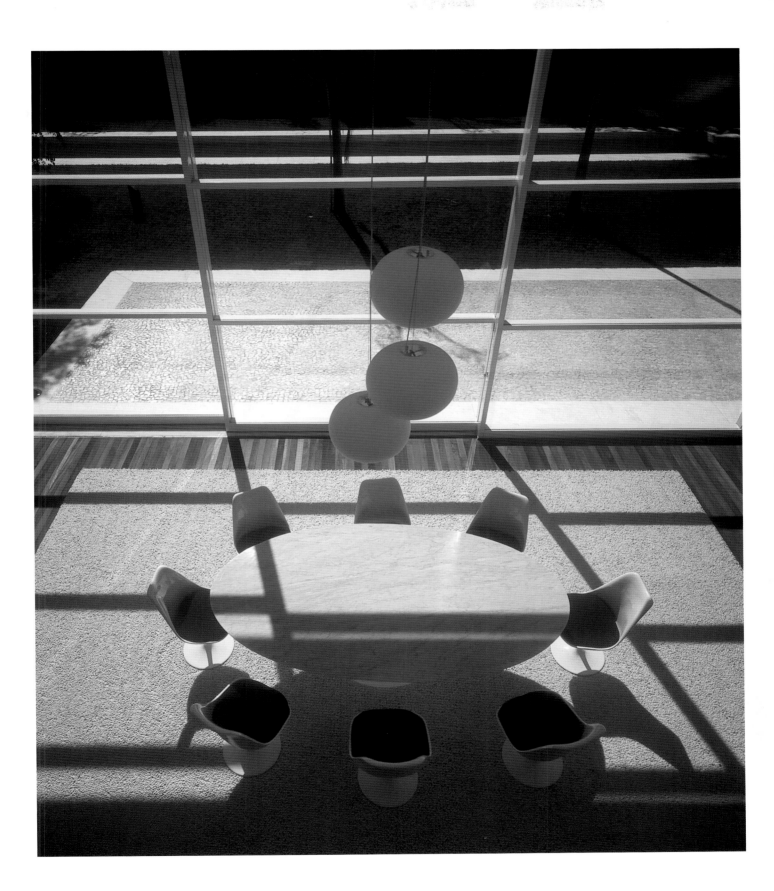

Marcio Kogan graduated from the Mackenzie School of Architecture in 1976. Since that time he has received many awards for different architectural assignments. He has designed a variety of small-scale and large-scale projects, mainly in São Paulo, Brazil and the surrounding area. His architectural work is known for its strong, refined lines. Since 1974 he combines architecture projects with his passion for the cinema. He has created a great number of short films, and his first full-length movie was made in 1988.

Marcio Kogan, diplômé en 1976 de l'école d'architecture Mackenzie, a obtenu de nombreux prix pour ses différentes réalisations. Il a dessiné des projets très variés, à petite et grande échelle, essentiellement à Sao Paolo (Brésil) et dans ses environs. Son travail d'architecte est reconnu pour la force et le raffinement de ses lignes. Depuis 1974, il associe à l'architecture sa passion du cinéma. Il a tourné nombre de courts métrages, et réalisé son premier long métrage en 1988.

Marcio Kogan schloss sein Studium 1976 an der Mackenzie School of Architecture ab und ist seitdem mit zahlreichen Preisen für seine Arbeiten ausgezeichnet worden. Er hat eine ganze Reihe kleiner und großer Gebäude hauptsächlich in São Paulo, Brasilien, und Umgebung entworfen. Seine Arbeit als Architekt ist vor allem von der Klarheit und Überzeugungskraft seiner Entwürfe gekennzeichnet, die er seit 1974 mit seiner Leidenschaft für das Kino kombiniert. Er hat für eine ganze Reihe von Kurzfilmen und auch bereits 1988 für einen Spielfilm Regie geführt.

According to the architects, this house is the result of an in-depth exploration of the different ways of relating to the views — those of the house as well as those that can be seen from it. The project is located on an elevated site with a view of the city of Melbourne on one side and a view of the nearby suburbs on the other. The relevance of these two views is embodied in the house in the form of a break in the large copper façade, which also creates the dramatic feeling of the high interior ceiling. The subtle details of the layout create different kinds of relationships between the various rooms and between the interior and exterior as well. The two-level structure is supported by a large concrete shell, which acts as a base and as a transition to the ground. The pool, the garage, a wine cellar, a storage room, and the access ramp are all located inside this base. The main part of the building, which looks much lighter, is made of a wood and metal frame and very light covering materials that filter the natural light.

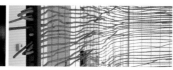

City Hill House

John Wardle Architects

Melbourne, Australia, 2003
Photos © Trevor Mein

29

Pour les architectes, cette maison résulte d'une étude approfondie des différentes manières de mettre en relation les vues, autant celles que l'on a de la demeure que celles qu'elle offre. Elle occupe une hauteur d'où l'on découvre, d'un côté la ville de Melbourne, de l'autre ses proches banlieues. L'axe et la pertinence de ces deux perspectives se manifestent dans la volumétrie de la construction, marquée par la rupture de la façade

Mit diesem Gebäude erforschten die Architekten verschiedene Methoden, um den Ausblick zu integrieren, sowohl innerhalb als auch außerhalb des Hauses. Das Gebäude befindet sich auf einem erhöhten Grundstück mit einem ausgezeichneten Blick über die Stadt Melbourne auf der einen Seite und auf die Vororte der Stadt auf der anderen. Die Achsen dieser beiden Faktoren wurden in der Volumetrie des Gebäudes so

principale, revêtue de cuivre, dont la vaste baie dramatise l'intérieur, élevé sur une double hauteur. Les subtils détails de la composition générale créent des différents types de relations entre les pièces comme entre l'intérieur et l'extérieur. La structure, à deux niveaux, repose sur un grand socle en béton qui joue le rôle à la fois de base et de liaison avec le terrain. Il abrite une piscine, un garage, un cellier, une pièce de rangement, accessibles par une rampe. Le volume principal, d'aspect beaucoup plus léger, est une structure en métal et bois supportant un revêtement très léger qui filtre la lumière naturelle.

umgesetzt, dass ein Bruch in der großen, mit Kupfer verkleideten Fassade entsteht, die gleichzeitig der doppelten Höhe im Inneren ihren dramatischen Charakter verleiht. Die leichten Drehungen im Gesamtbild schaffen verschiedene Beziehungen zwischen den einzelnen Räumen und zwischen innen und außen. Die zweistöckige Struktur stützt sich auf eine große Betonschale, die gleichzeitig die Basis und der Durchgang auf dem Grundstück ist. Darin befinden sich der Swimmingpool, die Garage, ein Weinkeller, ein Lagerraum und eine Zugangsrampe. Der Hauptteil des Gebäudes wirkt viel leichter und besteht aus einer Holz- und Metallstruktur, die als Rahmen für sehr leichte Verkleidungen dient, durch die sich das Tageslicht filtert.

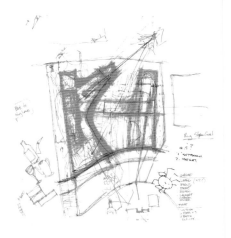

0   10   20

Ground floor

Rez-de-chaussée

Erdgeschoss

First floor

Premier étage

Erster Stock

Sketch

Esquisse

Skizze

1. What historical reference in particular inspires you when designing a residence?
Quelles références historiques vous inspirent en particulier lorsque vous dessinez une maison ?
Welche historische Referenz dient Ihnen als Inspiration beim Entwurf eines Hauses?

2. What is the main factor taken into consideration when designing a residence?
Quel facteur principal prenez-vous en considération lors de la conception d'une maison ?
Welche Rahmenbedingungen, bzw. Faktoren sind für Sie ausschlaggebend beim Konzipieren?

3. What room inside the home do you find most interesting to design?
Quelle pièce trouvez-vous la plus intéressante à dessiner ?
Welchen Raum des Hauses finden Sie am spannendsten zu entwerfen?

4. What is your criteria for choosing materials and finishings in a particular room?
Sur quels critères choisissez-vous les matériaux et les finitions d'une pièce ?
Welche Kriterien wenden Sie bei der Entscheidung über Materialien und Oberflächen in diesem Raum an?

1. The personal histories of our clients are intertwined with the history of the site, its physical characteristics, the region and its social history.

2. Each client and each site requires a unique response. The stage-management of views is always an important consideration.

3. Common to many of our projects is a notion of interrupting continuous space with devices and objects rather than compartmentalizing with walls.

4. The sensual aspect of materials and finishes, recognising the sense of touch in the process of design and manufacture. We aspire to create buildings that reflect the perception of our physical world in its vast and diverse phenomena, in the aesthetic experience of surface.

1. L'histoire personnelle de nos clients est tissée de l'histoire du lieu, de ses caractéristiques physiques, de la région et de son histoire sociale.

2. Chaque client et chaque site nécessitent une réponse unique. La mise en scène des vues, par exemple, est toujours une considération importante.

3. Tous nos projets s'appuient sur la notion d'un espace continu et interrompu seulement par des mécanismes ou des objets, plutôt que par des cloisons qui le compartimentent.

4. La sensualité des matériaux et des finitions, ainsi que leur aspect tactile lors de la conception et de la réalisation. Nous aspirons à créer des bâtiments qui reflètent, par une expérience esthétique des surfaces, la perception du monde physique dans l'immensité et la diversité de ses phénomènes.

1. Die persönliche Geschichte unserer Kunden verflechtet sich mit der Geschichte des Ortes, seinen physischen Eigenschaften, der Region und ihrer sozialen Geschichte.

2. Jeder Kunde und jeder Ort braucht eine einzige Antwort. Zum Beispiel der Umgang mit der Sicht, sowohl drinnen als auch draußen, ist ein wichtiger Gesichtspunkt.

3. Ein gemeinsamer Zug unserer Projekte ist die Vorstellung eines durchgehenden Raumes, der eher von Mechanismen und Objekten unterbrochen, als dass er durch Wände eingeteilt wird.

4. Das sinnliche Aussehen der Materialien und Oberflächen, wobei der Tastsinn im Gestaltungs- und Herstellungsprozess eine Rolle spielt. Wir versuchen, Gebäude zu schaffen, die unsere Wahrnehmung der physischen Welt und die große Vielfalt an Oberflächen widerspiegeln.

John Wardle Architects was founded in 1986, and at the present time it includes 21 professionals from diverse disciplines who collaborate on developing ideas for each project. The firm's uniqueness stems from the variety of projects that it has undertaken all over Australia. Their design portfolio includes single-family homes, apartment towers, university buildings, offices, and shopping malls. The architects work at incorporating the collective and individual characteristics of their clients to enrich and personalize every project.

Créée en 1986, l'agence John Wardle Architects regroupe aujourd'hui 21 professionnels de différentes disciplines qui collaborent au développement conceptuel de chaque projet. La particularité de l'agence tient à la diversité des projets qu'elle a réalisés dans toute l'Australie. Leur portfolio montre aussi bien des maisons individuelles, des appartements, des bâtiments universitaires, des bureaux que des centres commerciaux. Les architectes s'efforcent d'intégrer les spécificités collectives et particulières de leurs clients pour enrichir et personnaliser chaque projet.

Das Unternehmen John Wardle Architects wurde 1986 von Wardle selbst gegründet. Heute arbeiten 21 Fachleute verschiedener Disziplinen in diesem Büro, die gemeinsam Projekte entwickeln. Was dieses Unternehmen so besonders macht, ist die Tatsache, dass es in ganz Australien bereits sehr verschiedenartige Planungen durchgeführt hat. Dazu gehören Einfamilienhäuser, Mehrfamilienhäuser, Universitätsgebäude, Bürohäuser und Einkaufszentren. Die kollektiven und individuellen Eigenschaften jedes Kunden werden dazu benutzt, die einzelnen Projekte persönlicher zu gestalten und zu bereichern.

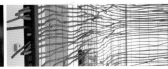

This house is located in Honda, Colombia. This dwelling is a combination of two properties facing the street that used to house residential and storage buildings. Only the façades and a few colonial period stonewalls were preserved and incorporated into the project. The climate is very hot year round because the city is at sea level and in the tropical zone. This second home for three associates was conceived as a sequence of open, covered spaces located inside the existing structure. The floor plan is based on sight lines, which convey a labyrinth-like feeling. Every room faces one of the exterior areas, each representing a particular theme: a patio with aromatic herbs, a garden of citrus trees, a rock garden, and a patio with red peppers. Water acts as a unifying element, in the form of a pool, a fountain, or a pond. The lighting, designed by Guillermo Arias, is a key element of the project, enhancing the character of the original walls, the textures, the vegetation, and the water elements.

House in Honda

Guillermo Arias + Luis Cuartas

Honda, Colombia, 2003
Photos © Eduardo Consuegra

Cette maison de Honda, en Colombie, est formée par la réunion de deux propriétés – une maison d'habitation et des entrepôts – donnant sur rue. Seules les façades et quelques murs en pierre de l'époque coloniale ont été conservés et incorporés au projet. Le climat de l'endroit, à peu près au niveau de la mer et dans une zone tropicale, présente des températures très élevées pendant toute l'année. Cette résidence secondaire pour

Dieses Gebäude befindet sich in Honda, Kolumbien. Dieses Haus entstand durch die Vereinigung zweier Parzellen, auf denen sich einst Wohn- und Lagerhäuser zur Straße hin befanden. Nur die koloniale Fassade und die Steinmauern sind erhalten und wurden in die Planung miteinbezogen. Da sich das Gebäude beinahe auf Höhe des Meeresspiegels und in einer Region mit tropischem Klima befindet, ist die Temperatur das ganze Jahr über

trois associés fut conçue comme une séquence d'espaces ouverts et couverts, créés à l'intérieur de l'existant, offrant une impression de labyrinthe qu'ordonnent les axes perspectifs. Les pièces sont toujours tournées vers un espace spécifique : une cour intérieure plantée d'herbes aromatiques, un jardin d'agrumes, un autre de pierres ou un patio de piments. L'eau – piscine, fontaines ou bassin – sert d'élément unificateur. Élément clé du projet, l'éclairage conçu par Guillermo Arias souligne le caractère des murs d'origine, des textures, de la végétation et des éléments aquatiques.

sehr hoch. Dieses Ferienhaus für drei Gesellschafter wurde als eine Sequenz von offenen und geschlossenen Räumen entworfen, die auf der bereits vorhandenen Struktur beruhen. So hat man das Gefühl, sich in einem Labyrinth zu befinden, das über visuelle Achsen geordnet ist. Alle Räume sind auf einen Gartenbereich mit spezifischem Charakter hin ausgerichtet: ein Innenhof mit Duft- und Würzkräutern, ein Garten mit Orangen- und Zitronenbäumen, ein Steingarten und ein Hof voller Pfeffersträuchern. Das Wasser dient als vereinigendes Element, in Form eines Swimmingpools, eines Brunnens und eines Teiches. Die Beleuchtung, die von Guillermo Arias entworfen wurde, ist ein entscheidendes Gestaltungselement, das den Charakter der alten Mauern, die Textur, die Vegetation und die Wasser-Elemente unterstreicht.

 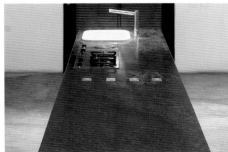

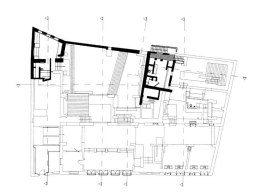

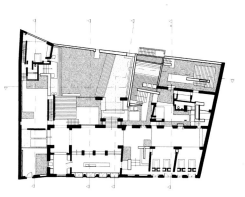

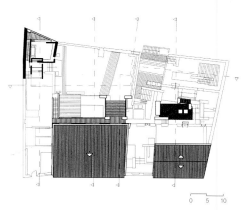

0   5   10

Ground floor

Rez-de-chaussée

Erdgeschoss

First floor

Premier étage

Erster Stock

Roof plan

Plan de toiture

Dachgrundriss

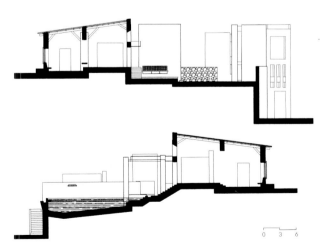

Sections
Coupes
Schnitte

0 3 6

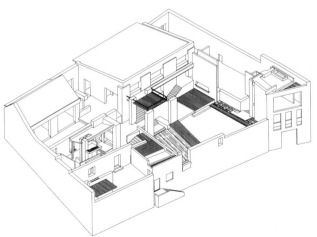

Axonometry
Axonométrie
Axonometrie

1. What historical reference in particular inspires you when designing a residence?
Quelles références historiques vous inspirent en particulier lorsque vous dessinez une maison ?
Welche historische Referenz dient Ihnen als Inspiration beim Entwurf eines Hauses?

2. What is the main factor taken into consideration when designing a residence?
Quel facteur principal prenez-vous en considération lors de la conception d'une maison ?
Welche Rahmenbedingungen, bzw. Faktoren sind für Sie ausschlaggebend beim Konzipieren?

3. What room inside the home do you find most interesting to design?
Quelle pièce trouvez-vous la plus intéressante à dessiner ?
Welchen Raum des Hauses finden Sie am spannendsten zu entwerfen?

4. What is your criteria for choosing materials and finishings in a particular room?
Sur quels critères choisissez-vous les matériaux et les finitions d'une pièce ?
Welche Kriterien wenden Sie bei der Entscheidung über Materialen und Oberflächen in diesem Raum an?

1. We do not use specific historic references when designing a residence. We are inspired as much by a Pompeian villa as by a modern house by Neutra or Mies van der Rohe.

2. The location and the requirements are the rational determining factors, while the pursuit of sensibility in the space is our personal approach.

3. The spaces that we consider most interesting are opposites, the most private ones and the ones that are most exposed and public. The former encourage intimacy and contemplation, while the more open living areas are the spatial culmination of the design process.

4. There are several aspects that influence the selection of materials: rational ones like the climate and the availability, and sensory ones like the feeling conveyed by the space.

1. Nous n'avons pas de références historiques particulières lors de la conception d'une résidence. Nous sommes tout autant inspirés par une villa de Pompéi que par une maison moderne de Neutra ou de Mies van der Rohe.

2. Le lieu et le programme sont des facteurs rationnels déterminants, mais notre approche personnelle s'appuie sur la quête de la sensibilité dans l'espace.

3. Les pièces que nous jugeons les plus intéressantes sont opposées : à la fois les plus intimes et les plus publiques. Les premières permettent recueillement et contemplation, tandis que nous considérons les secondes, par exemple les pièces de séjour, plus ouvertes, comme une conclusion spatiale de l'exercice de conception.

4. Plusieurs aspects nous influencent dans le choix d'un matériau : rationnels, en rapport avec le climat et la disponibilité, et sensoriels, c'est-à-dire ceux que révèle l'espace.

1. Wir haben keine konkrete historische Referenz bei der Planung eines Wohnhauses. Uns inspiriert eine pompejische Stadt genauso wie ein modernes Haus von Neutra oder Mies van der Rohe.

2. Der Ort und das Wohnprogramm sind die rationalen Gründe für die Entscheidung, während die Suche nach Sensibilität des Raumes unsere persönliche Suche ist.

3. Die Räume, die wir am interessantesten finden, sind in einer Art Gegenüberstellung die Räume, die am privatesten sind und die, die geteilt und gezeigt werden. In den ersten sucht man die Zurückgezogenheit und die Betrachtung, während in den anderen die Wohnbereiche offener sind. Diese verstehen wir als die räumliche Schlussfolgerung des gestalterischen Eingriffs.

4. Die Materialauswahl wird von verschiedenen Aspekten beeinflusst, rationale Aspekte wie das Klima und die Verfügbarkeit und emotionale Aspekte, die der Raum vermittelt.

Guillermo Arias was born in Bogota, Colombia. In 1986, he graduated as an architect from the Universidad de los Andes. That same year he founded the firm Octubre, where he designs various lighting projects and does architectural work. Since 2002 he has designed lamp collections for Goldsmith in New York.
Luis Cuartas was born in Medellin, Colombia. In 1990, he obtained a degree in architecture from the Universidad Javierana. Since then the two have collaborated on a wide variety of residential and commercial projects.

Né à Bogota (Colombie), Guillermo Arias est diplômé d'architecture de l'Universidad de los Andes depuis 1986. Cette même année, il créa l'agence Octubre, s'occupant de divers projets d'éclairage parallèlement à son travail d'architecte. Depuis 2002, il dessine les collections de lampes de la maison Goldsmith à New York.
Luis Cuartas est né à Medellin (Colombie) et est diplômé de l'Universidad Javierana depuis 1990. Depuis cette date, les deux architectes ont collaboré sur une grande variété de projets résidentiels et commerciaux.

Guillermo Arias kam in Bogotá in Kolumbien auf die Welt und machte 1986 sein Architekturdiplom an der Universität der Anden. Im gleichen Jahr gründete er das Unternehmen Octubre, in dem er verschiedene Beleuchtungsprojekte parallel zu seiner Arbeit als Architekt verwirklichte. Seit 2002 entwirft er die Lampenkollektion für Goldsmith in New York.
Luis Cuartas wurde in Medellín in Kolumbien geboren und schloss 1990 sein Architekturstudium an der Universität Javeriana ab. Seit diesem Jahr arbeiten die beiden Architekten an zahlreichen Bauprojekten für Wohn- und Geschäftshäuser zusammen.

The clients for this project, a couple with two children, were originally from the Philadelphia area. For the past ten years they have spent their summers on Long Beach Island, an island on the south coast of New Jersey. They were attracted to this property because of its solitary and comfortable character, lent by the area's dense woods. The clients not only wanted to maintain and protect this vegetation, but to make it an integral part of the project so they could enjoy it from within the living areas of the home. These concepts lead to the idea of placing the living quarters of the house on a higher level to create a more direct relationship with the vegetation. The more private areas, like the bedrooms, were placed on an even higher floor, above the trees and with a view of the ocean. The guest room, an office/gym, a storage room, and the building's entrance that faces the woods, are all on the ground floor. A metal framework reinforces the wooden structure and supports the large projections that emphasize the relationship with the surroundings.

Beach House

Christoff:Finio architecture

Long Beach Island, NY, USA, 2003
Photos © Elizabeth Felicella

Les clients de ce projet, un couple avec deux enfants, viennent de la région de Philadelphie. Passant tous les étés à Long Beach Island, une île située sur la côte sud du New Jersey, depuis dix ans, ils ont été séduits par cette propriété en raison de son confort et de l'isolement, que lui confère la forêt dense environnante. Les propriétaires ne désiraient pas seulement respecter et protéger la végétation mais l'intégrer également au

Die Auftraggeber für dieses Haus stammen aus der Gegend von Philadelphia. Es handelt sich um ein Paar mit zwei Kindern, die während der letzten 10 Jahre den Sommer auf Long Beach Island, einer Insel an der Südküste von New Jersey, verbracht haben. Dieses Haus inmitten eines dichten Waldes sagte ihnen aufgrund der zurückgezogenen und gleichzeitig einladenden Lage zu. Die Kunden wollten diesen Wald nicht nur erhalten und

projet afin d'en profiter depuis les pièces de séjour de la maison. Cette priorité a conduit à les aménager en étage en leur offrant un lien plus direct avec la végétation. Les pièces privées, comme les chambres, ont été aménagées à un niveau encore plus élevé, au-dessus des arbres et avec vue sur l'océan. La chambre d'amis, un bureau/salle de sport, une pièce de rangement, et l'entrée de la maison face à la forêt sont tous aménagés en rez-de-chaussée. Une charpente métallique renforce la structure en bois et supporte les parties en saillie qui accentuent la relation avec l'environnement.

beschützen, sondern ihn auch zu einem integralen Bestandteil der Planung machen, und ihn vom Wohnzimmer des Hauses aus genießen. Dadurch kam den Planern die Idee, die Wohnbereiche des Hauses auf einer etwas höheren Ebene anzulegen, um so eine direkte Beziehung zur Vegetation zu haben. Die privateren Räume wie die Schlafzimmer liegen auf einer noch höheren Ebene, über den Bäumen und mit Blick aufs Meer. Im Erdgeschoss befinden sich das Gästezimmer, ein Büro-Fitnessraum, ein Lager und der Zugang zum Haus, der sich zum Wald hin öffnet. Eine Metallstruktur verstärkt die Holzstruktur und stützt die großen Vorsprünge, die Beziehung zur Umgebung unterstreichen.

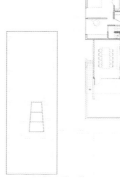

Ground floor
Rez-de-chaussée
Erdgeschoss

First floor
Premier étage
Erster Stock

Second floor
Deuxième étage
Zweiter Stock

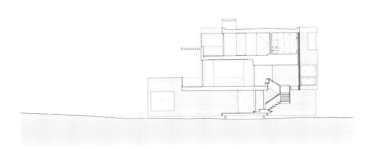

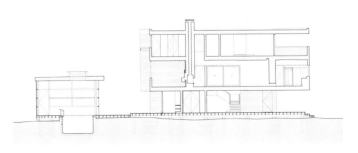

Sections

Coupes

Schnitte

0 2 4

1. What historical reference in particular inspires you when designing a residence?
   Quelles références historiques vous inspirent en particulier lorsque vous dessinez une maison ?
   Welche historische Referenz dient Ihnen als Inspiration beim Entwurf eines Hauses?

2. What is the main factor taken into consideration when designing a residence?
   Quel facteur principal prenez-vous en considération lors de la conception d'une maison ?
   Welche Rahmenbedingungen, bzw. Faktoren sind für Sie ausschlaggebend beim Konzipieren?

3. What room inside the home do you find most interesting to design?
   Quelle pièce trouvez-vous la plus intéressante à dessiner ?
   Welchen Raum des Hauses finden Sie am spannendsten zu entwerfen?

4. What is your criteria for choosing materials and finishings in a particular room?
   Sur quels critères choisissez-vous les matériaux et les finitions d'une pièce ?
   Welche Kriterien wenden Sie bei der Entscheidung über Materialien und Oberflächen in diesem Raum an?

1. The history of domesticity.

2. How to dignify living.

3. Any room that can extend outdoors.

4. Quiet innovation.

1. L'histoire familiale.

2. Comment donner de la dignité à une maison.

3. Toute pièce qui s'ouvre sur l'extérieur.

4. L'innovation tranquille.

1. Die Geschichte der Häuslichkeit.

2. Wie kann man eine Wohnung vergrößern.

3. Alle Räume, die sich nach außen öffnen.

4. Die maßvolle Innovation.

Martin Finio graduated from Cooper Union in New York. For ten years he was an associate architect in the office of Tod Williams and Billie Tsien, where he lead and participated in a wide variety of projects. He was the editor of the monograph "William Tsien: Works", and was a professor at Columbia and Yale Universities.
Taryn Christoff graduated from IIT and worked for several years in New York on large and small-scale projects, gaining experience in both corporate and residential projects. She founded the firm which Martin Finio would later join to create Christoff:Finio architecture.

Diplômé de la Cooper Union, à New York, Martin Finio a été pendant dix ans architecte associé dans l'agence de Tod Williams et Billie Tsien, où il a conduit et participé à de nombreux projets. Il a été l'éditeur de la monographie « William Tsien : Works », et fut professeur aux universités de Yale et de Columbia.
Taryn Christoff est diplômée de l'IIT et a travaillé pendant plusieurs années à New York sur des ouvrages d'échelles diverses, acquérant de l'expérience dans des projets de bureaux et de résidences. Elle a fondé l'agence que Martin Finio allait intégrer par la suite pour créer Christoff:Finio architecture.

Martin Finio studierte an der Cooper Union in New York und war 10 Jahre lang als assoziierter Architekt bei Tod Williams und Billie Tsien tätig, wo er an einer großen Reihe an Projekten teilnahm oder sie leitete. Er arbeitete als Herausgeber der Monographie „William Tsien: Works" und als Professor an den Universitäten von Columbia und Yale. Taryn Christoff schloss seine Studien an der IIT ab und arbeitete mehrere Jahre in New York, wo er Erfahrungen sowohl bei der Planung von Geschäfts- als auch Wohnhäusern sammelte. Er gründete die Firma, der später auch Martin Finio beitrat, und aus der dann Christoff:Finio architecture entstand.

This wood house, located in a rural area where stone is the principal construction material, was inspired by the agricultural buildings of the region. The architect defines the project as a granary for an artist because the house incorporates a working studio. The goal was to capture the best views of Lake Maggiore, so the building was designed in the form of a tower that was predominately vertical. The structural walls are made of concrete, while the interior walls are fabricated from insulated panels that are lighter and more flexible. The covering on the exterior, composed of narrow wood boards, emphasizes the verticality of the building even more, while a balcony that faces the west acts as a horizontal counterpoint. The location on the highest part of a hill represented a construction challenge because there was no existing entrance from the highway. As a result of this, the architects chose a prefabricated wood structure that was assembled in three days with the help of a helicopter.

Casa Larga

Daniele Claudio Taddei

Kloten, Switzerland, 2001
Photos © Bruno Helbling / zapaimages

Située dans une région rurale où la pierre est le principal matériau de construction, cette maison en bois s'inspire des bâtiments agricoles de la région. L'architecte définit le projet comme un grenier pour artiste, dans la mesure où la maison incorpore un atelier. L'idée première étant de pouvoir jouir des plus beaux panoramas sur le lac Majeur, le volume s'organise suivant un axe vertical en forme de tour. Les murs

Dieses Holzhaus, das in einem ländlichen Gebiet liegt, in dem hauptsächlich Steine als Baumaterial verwendet werden, ist von den Bauernhäusern der Region inspiriert. Der Architekt definiert das Gebäude als eine Scheune für einen Künstler, da es sich um ein Wohnhaus mit einem Atelier handelt. Von dem Gebäude aus sollte man einen der besten Panoramablicke auf den Lago Maggiore genießen, deshalb ist es vertikal wie ein Turm aufgebaut.

de refend sont en béton tandis que les cloisons qui divisent l'espace intérieur sont en panneaux isolants, ce qui autorise une flexibilité et une légèreté plus grandes. Le revêtement de la façade, réalisé en lattes de bois, accentue la verticalité du bâtiment, tandis qu'un balcon orienté à l'ouest sert de contrepoint horizontal. Le terrain étant situé au sommet d'une colline sans accès direct depuis la route, les architectes ont choisi une structure préfabriquée en bois qui fut assemblée en trois jours avec l'aide d'un hélicoptère.

Die tragenden Wände sind aus Beton, während die Zwischenwände im Inneren aus Isolierpaneelen sind, was die Gestaltung flexibler macht und dem Haus mehr Leichtigkeit verleiht. Die Fassade ist von außen mit Holzlatten verkleidet, was die vertikale Form noch unterstreicht. Ein Aussichtsbalkon mit Blick nach Westen dient als horizontaler Kontrapunkt. Der Standort oben auf einem Hügel war eine Herausforderung für die Planer, da es keine Zufahrt von der Landstraße aus gibt. Deshalb wurde das Gebäude mit einem Fertighaussystem aus Holz errichtet, das mit einem Hubschrauber transportiert und in drei Tagen montiert wurde.

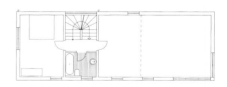

0 1 2

Ground floor

Rez-de-chaussée

Erdgeschoss

First floor

Premier étage

Erster Stock

Second floor

Deuxième étage

Zweiter Stock

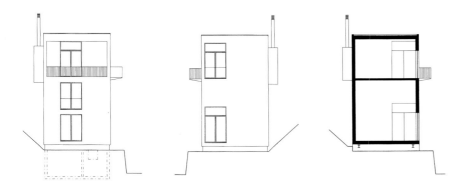
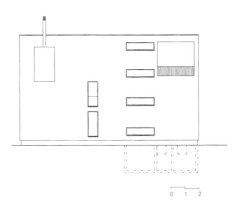

Sections

Coupes

Schnitte

Elevation

Élévation

Aufriss

Daniele Claudio Taddei was born in Lugano, Switzerland, in 1960. He pursued his early studies in Lugano and Tarasp, Switzerland, and continued with advanced studies in Stuttgart, Germany, graduating in 1986. He worked as an architect in several offices in Germany, Italy, the United States, and Switzerland. Since 2001 he has his own firm in Zurich, where he designs a variety of architecture and interior projects.

Daniele Claudio Taddei est né à Lugano (Suisse) en 1960. Il a fait ses études à Lugano et Tarasp (Suisse) puis les a poursuivies à Stuttgart (Allemagne), où il a été diplômé en 1986. Il a ensuite travaillé comme architecte dans plusieurs agences en Allemagne, en Italie, aux États-Unis et en Suisse. Depuis 2001, il possède sa propre agence à Zürich, où il s'occupe de nombreux projets d'architecture et de décoration.

Daniele Claudio Taddei kam 1960 in Lugano in der Schweiz auf die Welt. Nachdem er sein Studium in Lugano und Tarasp in der Schweiz begonnen hatte, setzte er es in Stuttgart in Deutschland fort, wo er 1986 sein Diplom erwarb. Er arbeitete als Architekt mit verschiedenen Architekturbüros in Deutschland, Italien, in den Vereinigten Staaten und in der Schweiz zusammen. Im Jahre 2001 gründete er seine eigene Firma in Zürich, mit der er eine Vielzahl von Projekten in den Bereichen Architektur und Innenarchitektur durchführt.

The main challenge of this project was designing a house that would take full advantage of the many views, while maintaining the privacy of its occupants and blending in with the surrounding environment. One part of the property faces the Andes mountain range including Cotopaxi, the highest snow-covered active volcano in Ecuador. The architects Wood + Zapata designed a house that was adapted to the site's mountainous terrain. The two main wings of the building form a large angle, allowing them to take in most of the views and create a feeling of proximity. A projecting terrace on the main wing of the house extends from the dining room towards Cotopaxi. The other wing ends at a road that borders the mountain and the swimming pool, which also extends outwards from inside the building. The façade that faces the mountain is almost entirely covered with green-colored glass, so one can always enjoy the view from the inside. From the outside the house blends into the landscape when viewed from across the valley.

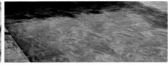

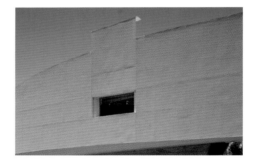

House in Miravalle

Wood + Zapata

Miravalle, Ecuador, 2002
Photos © Undine Pröhl

La principale gageure de ce projet était de concevoir une maison qui tire parti du panorama tout en conservant leur intimité à ses occupants et qui s'intègre à son environnement. En effet, une partie de la propriété fait face à la chaîne des Andes et au Cotopaxi, le plus haut volcan actif d'Équateur. Les architectes Wood + Zapata ont donc dessiné une maison adaptée à la nature montagneuse et accidentée du site, dont les deux ailes prin-

Die große Herausforderung bei dieser Planung war es, ein Haus zu entwerfen, das die interessante Aussicht integriert, aber gleichzeitig die Privatsphäre der Bewohner schützt und sich der Umgebung anpasst. Von einer Seite des Grundstückes sieht man auf die Andenkette und den Cotopaxi, den höchsten aktiven Vulkan in Ecuador. Die Architekten Wood + Zapata haben das Haus an die bergige Landschaft angepasst. Die beiden Hauptflügel

cipales forment un grand angle qui ouvre sur le panorama tout en créant un sentiment de proximité. L'aile principale de la maison montre une terrasse en saillie qui part de la salle à manger dans l'axe du Cotopaxi. L'autre aile aboutit à un chemin de montagne et à la piscine, également prolongée depuis l'intérieur de la maison. La quasi totalité de la façade orientée vers la montagne est en vitrage coloré vert : cela permet aux occupants de profiter en permanence du panorama et, vue depuis l'autre côté de la vallée, de mieux intégrer la maison dans le paysage.

Die des Gebäudes bilden einen weiten Winkel, um die wundervolle Aussicht näher zu bringen und so weit wie möglich zu umfassen. Der Hauptflügel des Hauses läuft in eine Terrasse auf einem Vorsprung aus, der sich vom Esszimmer in der Achse bis zum Cotopaxi erstreckt. Der andere Flügel endet an einem Weg, der an dem Berg entlang führt und am Swimmingpool, der ebenfalls bis in das Innere des Hauses reicht. Die Fassade zum Berg hin besteht fast vollständig aus grünem Glas, so dass man vom Inneren aus ständig diesen überwältigenden Blick hat und von außen, von der anderen Seite des Tales aus betrachtet, verschwindet das Haus fast in der Landschaft.

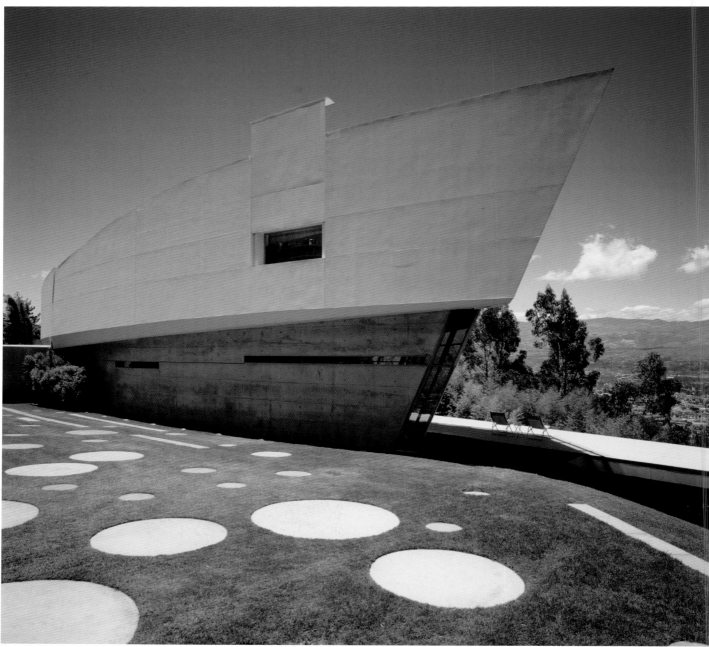

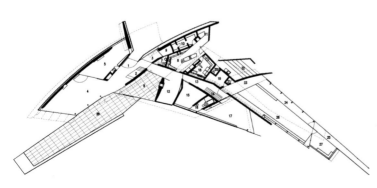

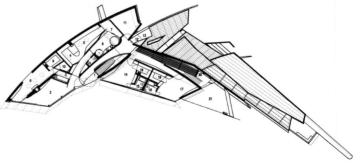

Ground floor
Rez-de-chaussée
Erdgeschoss

First floor
Premier étage
Erster Stock

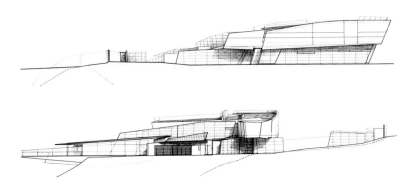

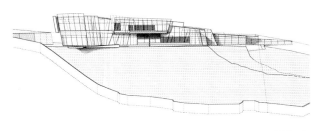

Elevations
Élévations
Aufrisse

Section
Coupe
Schnitt

1. What historical reference in particular inspires you when designing a residence?
Quelles références historiques vous inspirent en particulier lorsque vous dessinez une maison ?
Welche historische Referenz dient Ihnen als Inspiration beim Entwurf eines Hauses?

2. What is the main factor taken into consideration when designing a residence?
Quel facteur principal prenez-vous en considération lors de la conception d'une maison ?
Welche Rahmenbedingungen, bzw. Faktoren sind für Sie ausschlaggebend beim Konzipieren?

3. What room inside the home do you find most interesting to design?
Quelle pièce trouvez-vous la plus intéressante à dessiner ?
Welchen Raum des Hauses finden Sie am spannendsten zu entwerfen?

4. What is your criteria for choosing materials and finishings in a particular room?
Sur quels critères choisissez-vous les matériaux et les finitions d'une pièce ?
Welche Kriterien wenden Sie bei der Entscheidung über Materialien und Oberflächen in diesem Raum an?

1. There is no particular reference that applies to all residence projects. Obviously, there are masterfully executed houses that are part of the knowledge of every architect, such as the Schindler House, Falling Water, and works by Lautner. However, it is important to reconize the importance that the site has on the particular work.

2. Obviously the client. A custom designed residence should reflect the lifestyle of the person or family who commissions it. Equally important is the site and the climate in which it's built.

3. Each room is an element that completes the composition of the house. It's hard for me to pick one.

4. I use materials as providing color and texture as well as defining relationships between planes. However, in a house or room it is most important to create a warm balance between all the materials.

1. Aucune référence particulière ne peut s'appliquer à tous les projets résidentiels. Évidemment, il y a ces maisons magistralement conçues que chaque architecte connaît, comme la maison Schindler, la maison sur la Cascade et les œuvres de Lautner ; cependant, il est important de reconnaître l'importance qu'a le site dans la conception d'une œuvre particulière.

2. Évidemment le client. Une maison doit refléter le style de vie de la personne ou de la famille qui la commande. Mais le lieu et le climat sont également essentiels.

3. Chaque pièce est un élément qui vient compléter la composition de la maison. Il m'est difficile d'en privilégier une en particulier.

4. J'emploie des matériaux pour offrir une couleur et une texture et pour définir les relations entre les différents plans. Mais, qu'il s'agisse d'une maison ou d'une pièce, le plus important est de créer un équilibre chaleureux entre tous les matériaux.

1. Es gibt keine konkrete Referenz, die man auf alle Wohnprojekte anwenden kann. Offensichtlich gibt es perfekt geplante Häuser, an die jeder Architekt denkt, wie das Haus Schindler, und das Haus Wasserfall die Arbeiten von Lautner, dennoch ist es wichtig, an die Bedeutung des Standortes für eine konkrete Planung zu denken.

2. Natürlich der Kunde. Ein Haus sollte den Lebensstil einer Person oder einer Familie, die es sich bauen lässt, widerspiegeln. Das ist ebenso wichtig wie der Standort und das Klima der Umgebung.

3. Jeder Raum ist ein Element, das die Gestaltung des Hauses beeinflusst. Es ist schwierig, einen auszuwählen.

4. Ich benutze Materialien, die Farbe und Textur besitzen und die die Beziehungen zwischen den Ebenen definieren. Dennoch ist es in einem Haus oder einer Wohnung wichtig, ein warmes Gleichgewicht zwischen allen Materialien zu schaffen.

Since its inception in 1996, Wood + Zapata has made an effort to imprint its personal design perspective on each of the many different projects it has completed. These include the Chicago Bears Stadium, several private homes, spaces for commercial use, large-scale residential complexes, the new international terminal at the Miami airport, and the new construction and total rehabilitation of two blocks of the French historic center in Shanghai. From their offices in New York and Shanghai, they work on projects that range from master plans to furniture design.

Depuis sa création, en 1996, l'agence Wood + Zapata s'est efforcée d'imprimer sa perspective conceptuelle personnelle à chacun des nombreux projets qu'elle a réalisés. On peut citer notamment le stade des Chicago Bears, de nombreuses maisons individuelles, des espaces à usage commercial, de grands complexes résidentiels, le nouveau terminal international de l'aéroport de Miami, et la construction/réhabilitation de deux pâtés de maisons de l'ancien quartier français de Shanghai. Leurs agences de New York et Shanghai travaillent sur des projets qui vont du plan maître au design mobilier.

Seit der Gründung 1996 hat die Firma Wood + Zapata sich stets darum bemüht, ihre persönliche, architektonische Perspektive in jede ihrer Planungen einzubringen. Zu ihren Arbeiten gehören das Chicago Bears Stadium, viele Privat- und Geschäftshäuser, große Wohnkomplexe, das neue internationale Terminal am Flughafen von Miami und der völlige Um- und Neubau von zwei Häuserblöcken im historischen französischen Viertel von Shanghai. In ihren Büros in New York und Shanghai entwickeln sie Projekte, die von Masterplänen bis hin zum Möbeldesign reichen.

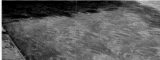

This house replaced one of the many modern homes built in the 1950's in Portola Valley, California. The neighborhood is characterized by well-groomed landscaping, a comfortable distance between buildings, and green areas that incorporate many walking trails. It was developed following the conventional notion of what constituted modern living during the middle of the last century. The architects were faced with the creation of a design that would fit in with the older existing environment and at the same time embody contemporary ideals. The clients, for their part, wanted a home that would incorporate attractive work areas. The design of the house, therefore, had to focus on both the public areas and those used for business meetings. The architects' response to these requirements was to articulate the public spaces, located on the lower level, and the private spaces in the upper floor, which are turned opposite those of the lower level to enjoy the view of the valley. The composition is based on a series of long, brightly colored walls that extend across the lot, with a few transversal planes that create a series of rooms that fulfill the requirements of the internal functions.

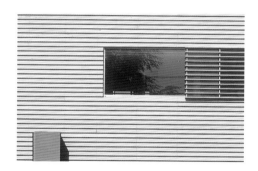

Castor Packard House

Callas Shortridge Architects

Portola Valley, CA, USA, 2002
Photos © Tim Griffith

Cette maison a remplacé une des nombreuses habitations modernes construites dans les années 1950 à Portola Valley, en Californie. Suivant les principes conventionnels du concept de vie moderne de l'époque, ce quartier se caractérise par un environnement soigné, qui assure une certaine distance entre les résidences, et des zones vertes sillonnées de chemins pédestres. Les architectes ont été confrontés au problème de

Dieses Haus befindet sich dort, wo eines der zahlreichen modernen Wohnhäuser aus den Fünfzigerjahren in Portola Valley, Kalifornien stand. Das Viertel zeichnet sich durch eine gepflegte Landschaft und einen relativ großen Abstand zwischen den einzelnen Häusern aus. Es gibt viele kleine Fußwege, die in die Natur führen. In dieser Umgebung, die nach den konventionellen Gesichtspunkten des modernen Lebens Mitte des vergangenen

réaliser un projet qui concilie le caractère ancien du bâti existant tout en témoignant d'idéaux contemporains. Les clients, quant à eux, désiraient une maison qui disposât d'espaces de travail accueillants. La réflexion devait par conséquent se concentrer à la fois sur les parties publiques et sur celles consacrées aux réunions de travail. La réponse a donc été d'articuler les espaces publics, situés à l'étage inférieur, et les espaces privés, concentrés à l'étage, suivant des orientations différentes afin que chacun profite de perspectives différentes sur la vallée. La composition se fonde sur une série de parois structurelles longitudinales de couleurs vives que croisent quelques plans transversaux en créant les pièces, et les fonctions internes, satisfaisant au programme.

Jahrhunderts entstanden ist, standen die Architekten vor der Herausforderung, ein Gebäude zu schaffen, das mit der Vergangenheit im Dialog steht und gleichzeitig die Kennzeichen der zeitgenössischen Landschaft aufweist. Die Kunden wünschten sich ein Wohnhaus mit komfortablen Arbeitsbereichen. Es mussten also öffentliche Bereiche und Orte für professionelle Zusammenkünfte geschaffen werden. Das Gebäude wurde so angelegt, dass sich die öffentlich genutzten Räume im Erdgeschoss und die privaten Wohnräume im Obergeschoss befinden, und zwar nach hinten, um den Panoramablick auf das Tal zu integrieren. Die Gestaltung wird durch eine Reihe von strukturellen, längs verlaufenden Wänden in lebendigen Farben geprägt, die am ganzen Grundstück entlang führen, während bestimmte quer verlaufende Ebenen Sequenzen von Räumen sind, die für verschiedene Funktionen bestimmt sind.

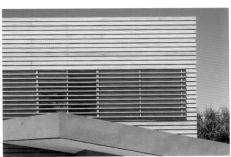

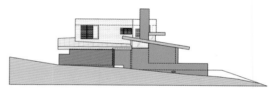

Elevations
Élévation
Aufrisse

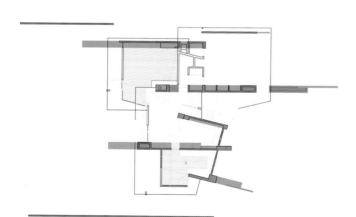

Ground floor
Rez-de-chaussée
Erdgeschoss

First floor
Premier étage
Erster Stock

0   2   4

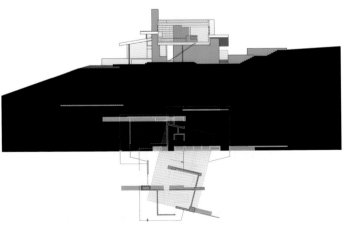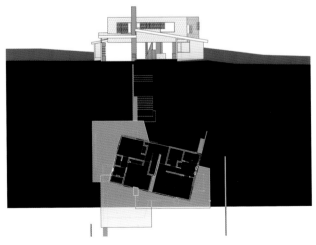

Sections

Coupes

Schnitte

0   4   8

The architectural firm of Callas Shortridge Architects has been in existence since 1996. Their founders, Steven Shortridge and Barbara Callas were architects at Israel Design Associates of Beverly Hills. Before starting their own office, the two worked together as project architects on a wide range of assignments of different scales. Barbara heads the development of projects that require detailed technical knowledge. Steven leads and manages the design and construction process for the firm's different projects. Both have received many prestigious awards for their design work.

Callas Shortridge Architects existe depuis 1996. Ses fondateurs, Steven Shortridge et Barbara Callas, furent tous deux architectes associés chez Israel Design Associates à Beverly Hills. Avant de créer leur propre agence, ils travaillèrent tous deux comme chefs de projet sur différentes réalisations de plus ou moins grande échelle. Barbara dirige le développement de projets qui nécessitent des compétences techniques, tandis que Steven dirige et gère la conception et les chantiers des différents projets de l'agence. Tous deux ont reçu nombre de prestigieuses récompenses pour leur œuvre.

Callas Shortridge Architects existiert seit dem Jahr 1996. Die Gründer Steven Shortridge und Barbara Callas waren vorher als assoziierte Architekten bei Israel Design Associates in Beverly Hills tätig. Bevor sie ihr eigenes Architekturbüro ins Leben riefen, arbeiteten sie als Projektarchitekten an Planungen verschiedener Größenordnung mit. Barbara überwacht die Projektabwicklung bei Planungen, für die ausgezeichnete technische Kenntnisse notwendig sind. Steven leitet den Gestaltungs- und Bauprozess für die veschiedenen Projekte des Unternehmens. Beide erhielten für ihr Werk bereits wichtige Designpreise.

This house is located in a suburb of the area of Boston, an area known for its low hills and a wide variety of residential construction. The clients are an older couple whose children no longer live with them, and who wanted a comfortable, functional, and adaptable home for their retirement. The wife's professional dedication to cooking largely determined the configuration of the residence and the importance of this activity within the house. The essential parameters of the design plan were dealing with the elongated shape of the property in combination with the steep angle of the terrain, the pursuit of views, and the difficulty of creating an access for vehicles. The resulting building has two levels; the bedrooms are located on the ground floor, and the main living space occupies the upper floor, which has the best views of the area. A functional look was given to the front elevation of the building that at the same time incorporates the symbolic and utilitarian presence of the automobile.

May Residence

Jonathan Levi Architects

Brookline, MA, USA, 1996
Photos © Anton Grassl / Jonathan Levi Architects

Cette maison est située dans une banlieue de Boston, une région caractérisée par ses douces collines et la diversité de ses constructions résidentielles. Les clients sont un couple âgé, désormais sans enfants, qui désirait une maison confortable, fonctionnelle et adaptable où se retirer. L'activité professionnelle de la femme – la cuisine – a déterminé en grande partie la configuration de la maison et l'importance accordée à cet espace.

Dieses Haus befindet sich in der Vorstadt von Boston in einer Region mit sanften Hügelketten und zahlreichen Wohnhäusern. Die Kunden sind ein älteres Paar mit erwachsenen Kindern, die nicht mehr zuhause wohnen. Sie wünschten sich eine komfortable, funktionelle und nicht allzu große Wohnung für ihren Lebensabend. Da die Dame des Hauses sich beruflich dem Kochen widmet, spielt die Küche innerhalb der Struktur des Hauses eine

Le projet s'est attaché en premier lieu à résoudre les problèmes dus à la forme allongée du terrain sur un terrain pentu, à la difficulté de créer un accès pour les véhicules et à l'ouverture de perspectives visuelles. La maison présente ainsi deux niveaux, avec les chambres en rez-de-chaussée et la salle de séjour principale à l'étage pour profiter du meilleur panorama. La façade principale présente un aspect fonctionnel qui intègre la présence utilitaire et symbolique de l'automobile.

große Rolle. Der Ausgangspunkt der Planung war es, eine Lösung für die relativ schwierige, längliche Form des Geländes mit starker Neigung zu finden, visuelle Höhepunkte und eine Zufahrt für Fahrzeuge zu schaffen. Das Gebäude besteht aus zwei Stockwerken, im Erdgeschoss befinden sich die Schlafzimmer und im Obergeschoss das Wohnzimmer, von dem aus man den besten Blick hat. Man versuchte, die Vorderfront einladend und wohnlich wirken zu lassen, aber gleichzeitig dort auch die symbolische und funktionelle Präsenz des Autos zu integrieren.

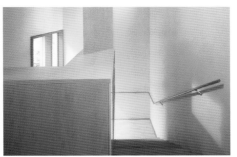

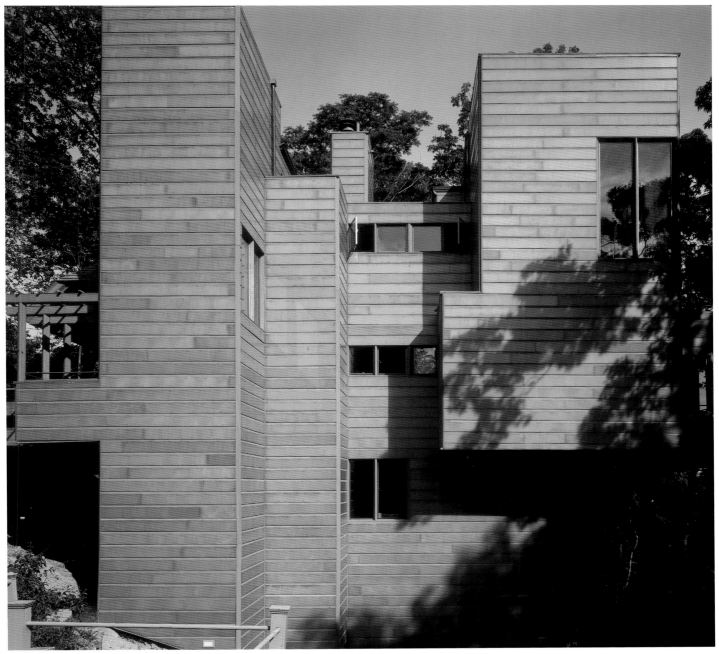

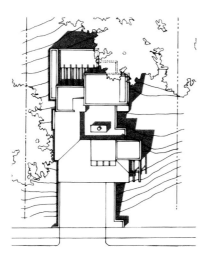

Roof plan

Plan de toiture

Dachgrundriss

First floor

Premier étage

Erster Stock

Second floor

Deuxième étage

Zweiter Stock

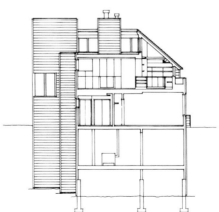

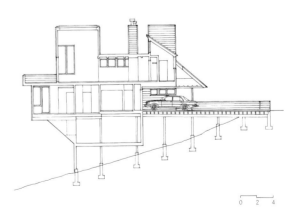

Transversal sections

Coupes transversales

Querschnitte

Longitudinal section

Coupe longitudinale

Längsaufriss

Jonathan Levi Architects is an architecture and interior design firm. Their buildings and interior spaces support and reinforce the highest aspirations of their clients. Their source of inspiration for every project stems from a comprehensive study of the conditions surrounding the individual project, and the close collaboration of the client. A rigorous design method based on the exploration of different alternatives guides their response to each design challenge. This results in conceptual clarity and the responsible use of resources.

Jonathan Levi Architects est une agence d'architecture et de décoration intérieure, qui s'attache à satisfaire les aspirations les plus élevées de ses clients. La source d'inspiration de chaque projet résulte d'une étude approfondie des circonstances qui entourent le projet individuel et de l'étroite collaboration du client. Leur méthode de conception rigoureuse, fondée sur l'exploration des différentes alternatives, guide alors leur réponse pour en assurer la clarté conceptuelle et une gestion responsable des coûts.

Jonathan Levi Architects ist ein Architektur- und Innenarchitekturstudio, das Gebäude und Innenräume plant, die den Wünschen und Bedürfnissen ihrer Kunden so weit wie möglich gerecht werden. Bei jeder dieser Planungen ist die Inspirationsquelle die enge Zusammenarbeit mit dem Kunden und eine genaue Analyse der Bedingungen jedes einzelnen Bauvorhabens. Die Antwort auf jede Situation entsteht aus der strengen und organisierten Planung der Gestaltung nach Überprüfung mehrerer Alternativen. So entstehen Gebäude mit niedrigen Kosten und einem klaren Konzept.

The C-House is a small yet complex urban building that is used for two different purposes: a residential studio and a commercial café, both of which belong to the same client. The place is on the outskirts of Tokyo, and it presented a difficult challenge because two major streets with heavy traffic surround the site. Rather than a simple juxtaposition of functions, combining the two designs was simply a reflection of Tokyo's contemporary urban lifestyle. Nowadays the private life of a resident of this city directly depends on the conditions of the city's public spaces. The line between what is private and what is public is becoming progressively blurred. The C-House is, therefore, an architectural materialization of this reality, and could be seen as a representation of the urban prototype in a single building. The transparent rooms of the café, located on the lower level and the terrace, literally wrap around the opaque volume that houses the private functions of the residence. The two sections of the project have independent access from the street, but at the same time they are connected internally, which emphasizes the flow between the two areas.

C-House

Toshimitsu Kuno, Nobuki Nomura / tele-design

Tokyo, Japan, 2002
Photos © Tatsuya Noaki, Tamotsu Matsumoto

La C-House est un bâtiment de petite taille mais complexe, qui associe deux programmes urbains différents: un appartement et un café, tous deux appartenant au même client. Située dans la banlieue de Tokyo, elle occupe un emplacement difficile au carrefour de deux rues à forte circulation. La conjonction des deux programmes, plus qu'une simple juxtaposition des fonctions, reflète simplement la vie urbaine contemporaine

Das Haus – C ist ein kleines, aber gleichzeitig sehr komplexes Gebäude, das zwei verschiedenen Zwecken dient, zum einen ist es ein Wohnatelier und zum anderen ein Café. Beide gehören dem Kunden selbst. Der Grundstück liegt am Stadtrand von Tokio und relativ ungünstig, da es von zwei viel befahrenen Straßen begrenzt wird. Diese Kombination zweier Funktionen, die nicht einfach nur in einem Nebeneinanderstellen besteht, ist lediglich eine

à Tokyo. Aujourd'hui, l'intimité d'un individu dans cette ville dépend directement de la nature de l'espace public. Les limites entre privé et public sont chaque jour plus estompées et confuses. La C-House est donc une matérialisation de cette réalité dans un bâtiment unique, qui peut alors se voir comme une représentation du prototype urbain. Les salles transparentes du café, en entresol et en étage, cernent littéralement le volume opaque qui abrite la partie privée résidentielle. Les deux parties disposent d'un accès indépendant depuis la rue tout en étant reliées intérieurement, ce qui met l'accent sur la circulation entre ces deux espaces.

Widerspiegelung des gegenwärtigen städtischen Lebens in Tokio. Das Privatleben eines Individuums in dieser Stadt hängt im steigenden Maße von den Bedingungen der öffentlichen Räume der Stadt ab. Die Grenzen zwischen privat und öffentlich werden immer instabiler, verwischter und sogar vorübergehend. Das Haus – C ist also die architektonische Materialisierung dieser Wirklichkeit und wird so zu einer Art urbaner Prototyp in einem einzigen Gebäude. Die transparenten Teile des Cafés im Erdgeschoss und das Flachdach umgeben die undurchsichtigen Gebäudeteile, in denen die Privaträume des Hauses liegen. Für beide Bereiche gibt es unabhängige Zugänge von der Straße aus, aber gleichzeitig sind sie miteinander verbunden, was den fließenden Übergang zwischen beiden Zonen noch unterstreicht.

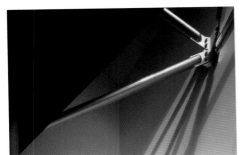
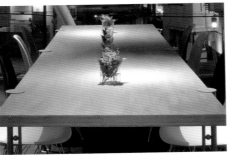

1. What historical reference in particular inspires you when designing a residence?
   Quelles références historiques vous inspirent en particulier lorsque vous dessinez une maison ?
   Welche historische Referenz dient Ihnen als Inspiration beim Entwurf eines Hauses?

2. What is the main factor taken into consideration when designing a residence?
   Quel facteur principal prenez-vous en considération lors de la conception d'une maison ?
   Welche Rahmenbedingungen, bzw. Faktoren sind für Sie ausschlaggebend beim Konzipieren?

3. What room inside the home do you find most interesting to design?
   Quelle pièce trouvez-vous la plus intéressante à dessiner ?
   Welchen Raum des Hauses finden Sie am spannendsten zu entwerfen?

4. What is your criteria for choosing materials and finishings in a particular room?
   Sur quels critères choisissez-vous les matériaux et les finitions d'une pièce ?
   Welche Kriterien wenden Sie bei der Entscheidung über Materialien und Oberflächen in diesem Raum an?

1. We explore flexible and transitive spatial condition in response to owners' needs. We try to understand the character of site as much as possible and then make it reflect on the positioning and composition of the residential space.

2. We don't design too much and try to leave the space in a condition into which the owners can intervene spontaneously.

3. Communal space rooms such as living room, dinning room and kitchen, because they allow various interaction among the family.

4. We make an effort to transform the owners' requests into appropriate materials in a specific and precise manner.

1. Nous étudions les conditions de flexibilité et de transition dans l'espace en réponse aux besoins du propriétaire. Nous essayons de comprendre le mieux possible le caractère du site pour qu'il reflète ensuite le positionnement et la composition de l'espace résidentiel.

2. Nous n'intervenons pas beaucoup dans la conception et nous essayons de laisser l'espace dans un état qui permette au propriétaire d'intervenir spontanément.

3. Les espaces publics, comme la salle de séjour, la salle à manger et la cuisine, car ils permettent des interactions diverses entre les membres de la famille.

4. Nous nous efforçons de satisfaire de manière spécifique et précise les demandes du propriétaire par des matériaux adaptés.

1. Wir erforschen die Bedingungen der Flexibilität und des Übergangs des Raumes und versuchen damit, den Bedürfnissen des Eigentümers zu entsprechen. Wir versuchen, die Eigentümlichkeiten des Ortes so gut wie möglich zu verstehen, um sie dann in der Lage und Anordnung des Wohnhauses oder der Wohnung widerzuspiegeln.

2. Wir greifen zurückhaltend ein. Wir möchten den Raum so lassen, dass auch die Eigentümer spontane Eingriffe vornehmen können.

3. Die von allen genutzten Räume wie das Wohnzimmer, das Esszimmer und die Küche, da es die Räume sind, in denen das Familienleben stattfindet.

4. Wir versuchen, die geeigneten Materialien präzise und spezifisch für die Bedürfnisse des Kunden auszuwählen.

Tele-design was established with the purpose of incorporating two important tendencies of contemporary Japanese society into the vision and structure of the company. The first was the pursuit of new models of economic growth, and the second was the rapid development of telecommunications within the global economy. In this way design becomes a tool for exploration as well as a vehicle for the incorporation of the latest technologies. Tele-design consists of a multi-disciplinary team that has worked together since 1999. Its unique structure has caught the attention of clients, the press and international critics.

Tele-design a été créé avec l'objectif d'associer dans la structure de l'agence deux tendances significatives de la société japonaise contemporaine. La première est la poursuite de nouveaux modèles de croissance économique, la seconde est le développement rapide des télécommunications au sein d'une économie globale. Ainsi, la conception devient un outil d'intégration des dernières technologies. Tele-design se compose d'une équipe pluridisciplinaire dont les membres travaillent ensemble depuis 1999. Cette structure particulière a attiré l'attention des clients, de la presse et de la critique internationale.

Tele-design wurde gegründet, um zwei wichtige Tendenzen der heutigen japanischen Gesellschaft in die Unternehmensstruktur zu integrieren. Diese Tendenzen sind die Suche nach neuen Modellen nach dem starken Wirtschaftswachstum und die schnelle Entwicklung der Telekommunikationen in der globalen Wirtschaft. So wurde das Design zu einem Werkzeug, um die neusten Technologien zu erforschen und sich von ihnen zu nähren. Tele-design arbeitet daher seit 1999 mit einem multidisziplinäres Team. Diese besondere Struktur erweckte viel Aufmerksamkeit seitens der Kunden und der internationalen Presse und Kritik.

This house is located in Mt. Washington, a diverse neighborhood sitting on the rolling hills very near the center of Los Angeles. Designed as a residence for the architects themselves, it is constructed around a concrete and steel modular framework. They conceived the house as a flexible and expandable environment that would evolve according to their future requirements. The most important considerations of the design were natural light, the connections between the spaces, and the relationship between the interior and the exterior. Both the budget and conservation of the natural environment were important considerations.

The project was optimized by constructing only what was necessary. The outdoor areas of this house were treated as extensions of the interior spaces, the traffic areas fulfill a double function, and the garage and attic were designed to house other functions in the future. By making full use of the possible extensions towards the outdoors and reducing the unused space to a minimum they achieved a modestly sized yet functional building. The interior design of the house was based on the relationships between the spaces, which were emphasized with bright and contrasting colors.

Fung + Blatt House

Fung + Blatt Architects

Los Angeles, CA, USA, 2003
Photos © Deborah Bird

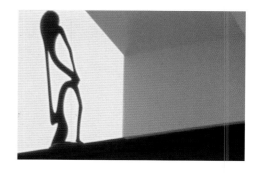

Cette maison, destinée aux architectes eux-mêmes, est située à Mt. Washington, un quartier hétérogène qui occupe les douces collines des environs immédiats du centre de Los Angeles. Construite autour d'un cadre modulaire en béton et acier, la maison est conçue comme un environnement flexible et expansible capable d'évoluer suivant les futurs besoins de ses occupants. La lumière naturelle, les connexions spatiales et la rela-

Das Haus befindet sich in Mt. Washington in einem sehr vielseitigen Stadtteil zwischen sanften Hügeln ganz in der Nähe vom Zentrum Los Angeles. Das Wohnhaus wurde von den Architekten selbst entworfen und umgibt ein modulares Grundgerippe aus Beton und Stahl. Sie entwarfen ihr Haus als eine flexible und dehnbare Umgebung, die sich mit den zukünftigen Bedürfnissen weiterentwickeln kann. Das Tageslicht, die Verbindungen

tion entre intérieur et extérieur ont été des considérations primordiales lors de la conception, et le projet a été optimisé en ne construisant que le nécessaire. Ici, les parties extérieures sont des prolongements de l'espace intérieur, les zones de circulation remplissant une double fonction, tandis que le garage et l'étage d'attique sont étudiés pour pouvoir servir d'autres types de fonctions à l'avenir. En exploitant au maximum les extensions possibles vers l'extérieur et en réduisant au minimum l'espace inutile, les architectes ont réussi un bâtiment de dimensions modestes mais fonctionnel. La décoration intérieure s'appuie sur les relations entre les espaces, mis en valeur par des couleurs vives et contrastées.

zwischen den Räumen und die Beziehung zwischen außen und innen spielten eine besonders große Rolle bei der Planung. Andere praktische Überlegungen mit gleichem Stellenwert sind die Kosten und der behutsame Umgang mit der Umwelt. Deshalb wurde die Planung optimiert, indem nur das wirklich Notwendige gebaut wurde. In diesem Haus sind die Außenbereiche eine Verlängerung der Innenräume, die Flure und Wege erfüllen eine doppelte Funktion und die Garage und der Dachraum sind so ausgelegt, dass sie in der Zukunft auch anderen Zwecken dienen können. Durch die Maximierung der Erweiterungen nach außen und Minimierung des nicht genutzten Raumes entstand ein Gebäude, das bescheiden und gleichzeitig sehr funktionell ist. Das Gesamtbild entstand durch ein abwechslungsreiches Spiel mit Formen und Baugruppen, die durch starke und kontrastierende Farben gegeneinander abgehoben sind.

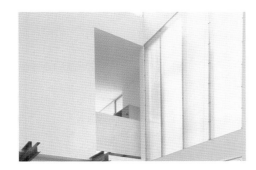

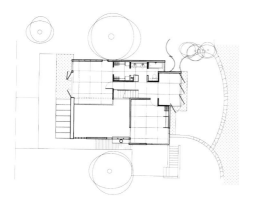

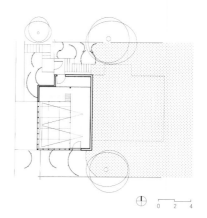

Ground floor

Rez-de-chaussée

Erdgeschoss

First floor

Premier étage

Erster Stock

Second floor

Deuxième étage

Zweiter Stock

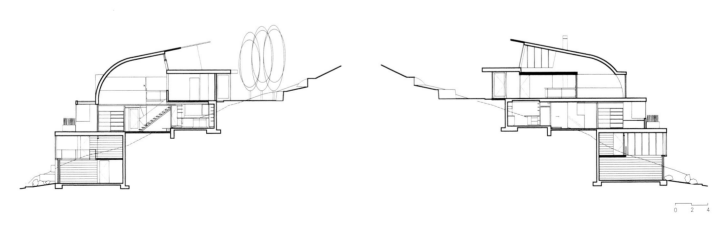

0 2 4

Sections

Coupes

Schnitte

1. What historical reference in particular inspires you when designing a residence?
Quelles références historiques vous inspirent en particulier lorsque vous dessinez une maison ?
Welche historische Referenz dient Ihnen als Inspiration beim Entwurf eines Hauses?

2. What is the main factor taken into consideration when designing a residence?
Quel facteur principal prenez-vous en considération lors de la conception d'une maison ?
Welche Rahmenbedingungen, bzw. Faktoren sind für Sie ausschlaggebend beim Konzipieren?

3. What room inside the home do you find most interesting to design?
Quelle pièce trouvez-vous la plus intéressante à dessiner ?
Welchen Raum des Hauses finden Sie am spannendsten zu entwerfen?

4. What is your criteria for choosing materials and finishings in a particular room?
Sur quels critères choisissez-vous les matériaux et les finitions d'une pièce ?
Welche Kriterien wenden Sie bei der Entscheidung über Materialien und Oberflächen in diesem Raum an?

1. We look at the history of the context, for traces of what came before. We may find and build upon a salient part of that memory, not in a sentimental or representational way, but by an abstraction of or an enactment of it.

2. In our design, the choreography of the human experience precedes the genesis of form.

3. We find interstitial spaces, such as the residual plazas and paseos left from the figure of the buildings to be some of the most interesting places of an urbanscape.

4. We believe in the responsible use of resources, and in the expression of material and structure as an integral part of how the environment is made. Materials can be a kind of chronicle of the building's making; from the concrete foundation walls, the heavy steel structure, the light gauge steel skeleton, the flesh of the plastered walls to infill of the cabinetry and partitions.

1. Nous prenons en compte l'histoire de l'environnement, cherchant des traces de ce qui préexistait. Une fois trouvées, nous pouvons construire sur ce qui émerge de cette mémoire, pas d'une manière sentimentale ou représentationnelle mais par abstraction ou recréation.

2. Dans notre conception, la chorégraphie de l'expérience humaine précède la genèse de la forme.

3. Nous trouvons que les espaces interstitiels, comme les places et les promenades nées des édifices, sont les lieux les plus intéressants du paysage urbain.

4. Nous croyons en l'emploi responsable des ressources, et pensons que l'expression de la matière et de la structure fait partie intégrante de la manière dont est fait l'environnement. Les matériaux peuvent être une sorte de chronique de la construction du bâtiment ; depuis les murs de fondation en béton, la lourde structure en métal, la légère charpente en acier jusqu'aux cloisons de plâtre qui définissent le mobilier et les intérieurs.

1. Wir beachten stets die Geschichte des Kontexts. Es ist möglich, dass wir Spuren finden und dass der Bau von dieser Erinnerung ausgeht, aber nicht auf sentimentale oder figurative Weise, sondern durch die Abstraktion und Nachahmung der Vergangenheit.

2. In unseren Entwürfen geht der Choreographie der menschlichen Erfahrung die Entstehung der Form voraus.

3. Die Räume wie die Plätze und Gänge, die von den Formen der Gebäude getrennt sind, sind für uns die interessantesten Orte innerhalb der Stadtlandschaft.

4. Für uns ist der verantwortungsvolle Einsatz von Mitteln und die Ausdrucksfähigkeit des Materials und der Struktur als integraler Bestandteil unserer Umgebung von großer Bedeutung. Die Materialien können eine Art Chronik das Baus darstellen, angefangen bei dem Fundament aus Beton, der schweren Metallstruktur, dem leichten Stahlskelett bis hin zu den Gipswänden, in denen Möbel und die Unterteilungen untergebracht sind.

Fung + Blatt Architects, founded in 1990 by Alice Fung and Michael Rosner Blatt, is a firm with five people dedicated to designing residential, commercial, and community projects. Their background in structural design and art results in projects that maintain a balance among structure, architecture, and landscape. This multidisciplinary team believes that the group effort helps all the pieces of a project fit together. They are committed to using resources responsibly in a design that is adapted to the surroundings, that acknowledges the past, and that anticipates the changes in the future of each client.

Consacrée à la réalisation de projets résidentiels, commerciaux et communautaires, Fung + Blatt Architects est une agence de cinq personnes fondée en 1990 par Alice Fung et Michael Rosner Blatt. Leur formation en design structurel et artistique les conduit à une analyse des interactions entre structure, architecture et paysage. Le groupe croit qu'une équipe pluridisciplinaire contribue à assembler toutes les pièces d'une œuvre. Cela implique le souci d'un usage responsable des ressources et une conception adaptée à l'environnement, prenant en compte le passé et anticipant les évolutions de chaque client.

Fung + Blatt Architects wurde 1990 von Alice Fung und Michael Rosner Blatt gegründet. Es handelt sich um ein Unternehmen mit 5 Mitarbeitern, die sich dem Entwurf von Wohn-, Geschäfts- und Gemeinschaftsgebäuden widmen. Aufgrund ihrer Ausbildung im Bereich Architektur und Kunst ist die Grundlage ihrer Vorgehensweise eine permanente Analyse der Beziehung zwischen Struktur, Architektur und Landschaft. Sie glauben daran, dass durch die Summierung der Erfahrung und Arbeit eines multidisziplinären Teams ein Ergebnis erreicht wird, bei dem alle Teile in ein Gesamtwerk passen.

This house is located about 250 miles (400 kilometers) from São Paulo, Brazil, on a property with typically exuberant, tropical vegetation. The residence presents two sides that are clearly different yet complementary. From the outside it looks like an austere, contemporary building, but a glance at the exterior patio reveals a type of architecture with references that are clearly traditional. These two languages blend harmoniously, aided by the exterior landscape, which is always present in the home. The outside of the house is faced with mineira stone, which is typical of this region. The cement and natural stone floor, and the wood screens that let in the natural light, provide great warmth to the interior. The single-level home has an L-shape layout, and the peripheral wall on the other two sides defines the patio, which is faced by the bedrooms and the living room.

Du Plessis House

Marcio Kogan

São Paulo, Brazil, 2003
Photos © Arnaldo Pappalardo

Cette maison se trouve à 400 kilomètres de Sao Paolo (Brésil), sur un terrain à la végétation exubérante et typiquement tropicale. Elle présente deux aspects clairement différenciés et en même temps complémentaires. L'extérieur est celui d'un bâtiment austère et contemporain, tandis qu'on découvre avec le patio extérieur une architecture aux évidentes références traditionnelles. Ces deux langages se superposent harmonieuse-

Dieses Haus befindet sich 400 Kilometer von São Paulo, Brasilien, entfernt auf einem Grundstück mit einer üppigen, typisch tropischen Vegetation. Das Haus zeigt sich von zwei klar differenzierten Seiten, die sich gegenseitig ergänzen. Von außen handelt es sich um ein nüchternes und zeitgenössisches Haus, während ein Blick durch den Hof eine Architektur zeigt, die offensichtlich von der traditionellen Bauweise beeinflusst ist. Diese

ment grâce au paysage, omniprésent à l'intérieur de la maison. Le volume extérieur, revêtu de mineira, une pierre typique de la région, est un parallélépipède entourant le patio où se concentre toute la vie sociale de la maison. Le pavement de ciment et de pierre naturelle, ainsi que les claustras de bois qui filtrent la lumière naturelle, apportent une grande chaleur à l'intérieur. La maison, développée sur un seul niveau, présente un plan en L, où les chambres et la salle de séjour ouvrent sur le patio défini par le mur périphérique.

beiden Stile werden harmonisch mit einander kombiniert und durch eine Landschaft ergänzt, die auch im Haus immer präsent ist. Das Gebäude ist von außen mit Natursteinen aus Minas Gerais verkleidet, ein für diese Region typischer Stein, und formt einen Block, der einen Hof umgibt, zu dem hin die Wohn- und Aufenthaltsräume des Hauses liegen. Durch den Boden aus Zement und Naturstein und die Jalousien aus Holz, durch die sich das Tageslicht filtert, wirkt das Innere sehr warm. Das Haus besitzt nur ein Stockwerk und ist in L-Form angelegt. Die Schlafzimmer und das Wohnzimmer liegen zum Hof, der von einer Mauer umgeben wird.

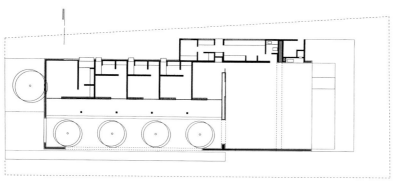

Ground floor

Rez-de-chaussée

Erdgeschoss

Side elevation

Élévation latérale

Seitenaufriss

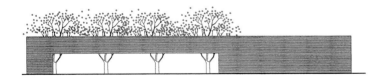

Elevations

Élévations

Aufrisse

Marcio Kogan graduated from the Mackenzie School of Architecture in 1976. Since that time he has received many awards for different architectural assignments. He has designed a variety of small-scale and large-scale projects, mainly in Sao Paulo, Brazil and the surrounding area. His architectural work is known for its strong, refined lines. Since 1974 he combines architecture projects with his passion for the cinema. He has created a great number of short films, and his first full-length movie was made in 1988.

Marcio Kogan, diplômé en 1976 de l'école d'architecture Mackenzie, a obtenu de nombreux prix pour ses différentes réalisations. Il a dessiné des projets très variés, à petite et grande échelle, essentiellement à Sao Paolo (Brésil) et dans ses environs. Son travail d'architecte est reconnu pour la force et le raffinement de ses lignes. Depuis 1974, il associe à l'architecture sa passion du cinéma. Il a tourné nombre de courts métrages, et réalisé son premier long métrage en 1988.

Marcio Kogan schloss sein Studium 1976 an der Mackenzie School of Architecture ab und ist seitdem mit zahlreichen Preisen für verschiedene seiner Bauten ausgezeichnet worden. Er hat eine ganze Reihe kleiner und großer Gebäude hauptsächlich in Sao Paulo, Brasilien, und Umgebung entworfen. Seine Arbeit als Architekt ist vor allem von der Klarheit und Überzeugungskraft seiner Entwürfe gekennzeichnet, die er seit 1974 mit seiner Leidenschaft für das Kino kombiniert. Er hat für eine ganze Reihe von Kurzfilmen und 1988 auch für einen Spielfilm Regie geführt.

This house is located in a residential suburb of Madrid on a generously sized lot. An initial decision was made to place the structure very near the access road to ensure the privacy of the larger part of the property. The general shape was designed like a geode, a natural hole in certain rocks lined with crystals. The building looks like a chunk of granite, solid, dense, and stone-like, contrasting with the large glass openings, which is an analogy of the crystallized part of this artificial geode. There are two levels above ground and a basement; the latter consists of a garage, a sunken patio, and the vertical passageway that leads to the upper levels. The main entrance, on the ground floor, is accessed from the carport. It is protected by an opening in the building that forms a low porch with an overhang. The living, dining, and bathrooms are on this level, which has a spectacular high ceiling. The upper level is used for the bedrooms.

Las Encinas Residence

Vicens + Ramos

Madrid, Spain, 2003
Photos © Eugeni Pons

Cette maison occupe un vaste terrain dans une banlieue résidentielle de Madrid. La première décision fut d'aménager le bâtiment le plus près possible de la rue afin d'utiliser en jardin la plus grande partie de la parcelle. Le volume général se présente comme un bloc de granite massif, solide et dense, que percent de larges baies, par analogie avec les cristaux qui tapissent une géode, ce trou naturel et cristallisé qu'offrent certaines

Das Haus befindet sich in einem Wohngebiet von Madrid auf einem großen Grundstück. Die erste Entscheidung, die man bei der Planung traf, war es, das Haus in der Nähe der Straße zu errichten und so einen Großteil des Grundstückes als Privatgarten nutzen zu können. Das Gebäude bildet eine Art Geode, eine natürliche Höhlung, die es in manchen Steinen gibt und die von einer kristallisierten Substanz umgeben ist. Das Gebäude hat einen

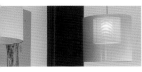    

pierres. La maison se développe sur deux niveaux et un sous-sol, où sont aménagés le garage, un patio et le vestibule vertical qui conduit aux étages supérieurs. L'accès principal du rez-de-chaussée se fait depuis le préau du parking extérieur, protégé par une ouverture dans le bâtiment qui forme un porche bas surplombé d'un saillant. Cet étage, d'une extraordinaire pleine hauteur, est occupé par les espaces de séjour, la salle à manger et les salles de bains. L'étage supérieur est réservé aux chambres.

massiven, geschlossenen, steinernen Granitkörper, der einen Gegensatz zu den großen, verglasten Öffnungen bildet, eine Analogie zu dem kristallinen Teil dieser künstlichen Geode. Das Haus hat zwei Stockwerke auf einem Gefälle und ein Kellergeschoss, in dem sich die Garage, ein in den Boden eingelassener Hof und eine vertikale Eingangshalle befinden, die in die oberen Stockwerke führt. Der Haupteingang durch das Erdgeschoss liegt im Hof des Parkplatzes und ist wie eine Ausgrabung am Gebäude, eine Art niedrige Vorhalle angelegt. Im Erdgeschoss liegen das Wohn- und Esszimmer, die Bäder und außerdem ein beeindruckender Raum mit doppelter Höhe. Im Obergeschoss befinden sich die Schlafzimmer.

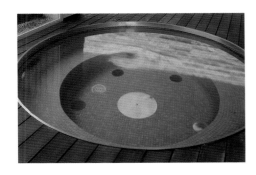

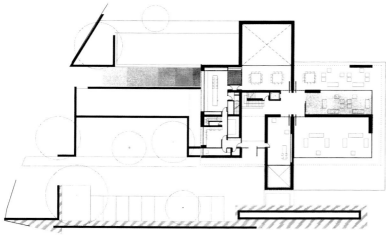

Ground floor

Rez-de-chaussée

Erdgeschoss

First floor

Premier étage

Erster Stock

0   3   6

Elevation

Élévation

Aufriss

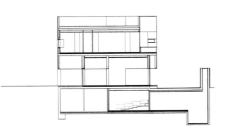

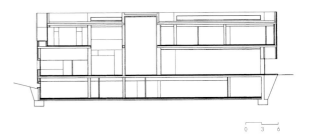

Sections

Coupes

Schnitte

0 3 6

1. What historical reference in particular inspires you when designing a residence?

   Quelles références historiques vous inspirent en particulier lorsque vous dessinez une maison ?

   Welche historische Referenz dient Ihnen als Inspiration beim Entwurf eines Hauses?

2. What is the main factor taken into consideration when designing a residence?

   Quel facteur principal prenez-vous en considération lors de la conception d'une maison ?

   Welche Rahmenbedingungen, bzw. Faktoren sind für Sie ausschlaggebend beim Konzipieren?

3. What room inside the home do you find most interesting to design?

   Quelle pièce trouvez-vous la plus intéressante à dessiner ?

   Welchen Raum des Hauses finden Sie am spannendsten zu entwerfen?

4. What is your criteria for choosing materials and finishings in a particular room?

   Sur quels critères choisissez-vous les matériaux et les finitions d'une pièce ?

   Welche Kriterien wenden Sie bei der Entscheidung über Materialien und Oberflächen in diesem Raum an?

1. The architect works from memory. Not just based on history, but drawing selectively and critically from his or her knowledge of history. Therefore, all previous experience is reference material for projects. From this premise, as Quaroni said, history becomes a tool, knowledge of which is indispensable, but once you know it, it cannot be used without interpretation.

2. Architecture is a problem of proportion and balance. There is no single determinant factor but many, whose simultaneous consideration is essential. Good architecture is always complex and satisfies a myriad of functional, design, cultural requirements at the same time.

3. Every room is important and interesting from the standpoint of the house as a whole, as a setting for relationships among the family members, and between them and society.

4. There is no single, previously existing criterium, but criteria that depend on a multitude of factors.

1. L'architecte travaille à partir de la mémoire. Pas seulement celle de l'Histoire mais aussi celle née de l'élaboration critique et sélective de ses connaissances historiques. Ainsi, toute expérience précédente est une référence au projet. Partant de ce postulat, comme dit Quaroni, l'Histoire devient un outil dont la connaissance est indispensable mais qui, une fois qu'on la possède, ne peut être employée sans interprétation.

2. L'architecture est un problème de proportions et d'équilibres. Il n'y a pas un facteur déterminant, sinon beaucoup, dont la considération simultanée est essentielle. La bonne architecture est toujours complexe et satisfait à la fois des multitudes de besoins fonctionnels, programmatiques, culturels, etc.

3. Dès lors qu'on considère la maison comme un ensemble, comme un lieu global de relations familiales, toutes les pièces sont également intéressantes et importantes.

4. Il n'y a pas un critère préalable mais des critères qui dépendent d'une multitude de facteurs.

1. Der Architekt entwirft aus dem Gedächtnis. Dabei beruft er sich nicht nur auf die Geschichte, sondern auch auf die kritische und selektive Ausarbeitung seiner historischen Kenntnisse. Deshalb ist jegliche Erfahrung eine Referenz für die Planung.

2. Die Architektur ist ein Problem von Proportionen und Gleichgewichten. Es gibt nicht einen entscheidenden Faktor, sondern viele. Es ist wichtig, sie alle gleichzeitig zu betrachten. Eine gute Architektur ist immer komplex und entspricht gleichzeitig einer Vielzahl von funktionellen, programmatischen, kulturellen, technischen und umweltbedingten Anforderungen.

3. Wenn man eine Wohnung als ein Ganzes betrachten, als eine globale Umgebung für die familiären Beziehungen und der Beziehungen der Familie zur Gesellschaft, dann sind alle Räume gleich interessant und wichtig.

4. Es gibt kein Kriterium, das schon vorher feststeht, sondern nur Kriterien, die von einer Vielzahl von Faktoren abhängen.

The architecture studio of Vicens + Ramos has been active since 1984. Ignacio Vicens and Hualde is a Professor of Planning in the School of Architecture in Madrid, where he is also the Assistant Director of Doctoral Research and Postgraduate Studies. José Antonio Ramos Abengózar is a Professor of Planning in the same school. The focus of the studio is a combination of professional activity and teaching, which leads to continuous research that feeds the design process. The firm has received numerous awards in Spain for a wide range of projects.

L'agence d'architecture Vicens + Ramos existe depuis 1984. Ignacio Vicens y Hualde est professeur de gestion de projet et directeur adjoint responsable des doctorats, de la recherche et du troisième cycle à l'école d'architecture de Madrid. José Antonio Ramos Abengozar est professeur de gestion de projet dans la même école. La combinaison entre activité professionnelle et enseignement académique définit l'orientation de l'agence vers une recherche permanente qui alimente le processus de conception. Elle a obtenu de nombreux prix en Espagne pour plusieurs de ses réalisations.

Das Architekturbüro Vicens + Ramos besteht seit 1984. Ignacio Vicens y Hualde ist Professor im Bereich Planung an der Architekturschule von Madrid, an der er auch gleichzeitig stellvertretender Direktor für die Dissertationen, Forschung und die postgraduierten Studien ist. José Antonio Ramos Abengózar ist Professor im Bereich Planung an der gleichen Fachhochschule. Diese akademische Lehrtätigkeit prägt auch die Arbeit des Unternehmens, in dem die ständige Forschung die Grundlage für den Gestaltungsprozess bildet. Dem Unternehmen wurden zahlreiche spanische Preise für mehrere Gebäude verschiedener Art verliehen.

The design of this single-family home is based on the fact that today the city of Yokohama is considered one more suburb of the rapidly growing Tokyo metropolitan area. The property, despite being on a hill, has a strong urban feeling, yet it has no tendency towards a specific style. The design approach was based on a review of the conditions of the site and the creation of a series of functions related to each other and to the exterior. The L-shaped configuration allowed the creation of a versatile interior. The different terraces and spaces that face the patio, which resulted from the shape of the house, play off each other to create many scenarios and uses for each room. The extension of the interior spaces towards the outside terraces is emphasized by using the same materials and finishes in both. This approach also created a harmonious relationship between the interior environment and the general context of the neighborhood. From outside, on the other hand, the look proposed for the façade was one of enclosure and austerity to reflect the surrounding structures.

Double-L

Noriyuki Tajima / tele-design

Yokohama, Japan, 2002
Photos © Tatsuya Noaki

En raison de l'incroyable expansion de la zone métro-
politaine de Tokyo, la ville de Yokohama est aujourd'hui
considérée comme un quartier supplémentaire de la
capitale japonaise. Ce projet de maison individuelle se
fonde sur ce constat. L'emplacement du terrain, bien
que sur une colline, présente un caractère urbain mar-
qué sans aucun style spécifique. La proposition faite
reconsidère la situation du lieu et définit une séquence

Aufgrund des unglaublich schnellen Wachstums des
Stadtgebietes von Tokio kann man die Stadt Yokohama
heute fast als einen weiteren Vorort von Tokio betrachten.
Darauf basiert die Planung für dieses Einfamilienhaus. Es
befindet sich auf einem Grundstück, das zwar auf einem
Hügel gelegen ist, aber trotzdem einen sehr städtischen
und relativ gewöhnlichen Charakter hat. Diese durch das
Grundstück vorgegebenen Bedingungen beeinflussten die

d'activités liées entre elles et avec l'extérieur. La forme
en L de la composition générale permet de créer un
monde intérieur dans lequel les multiples terrasses et
espaces qui regardent le patio généré par cette forme
sont liés entre eux, offrant une grande diversité de
situations et de nombreuses manières d'appréhender
chaque pièce de la maison. Le prolongement des espaces intérieurs vers les terrasses extérieures est souli-
gné par l'utilisation de matériaux et de finitions identiques. Cette approche propose également une relation
harmonieuse entre l'environnement intérieur et le
contexte général du voisinage. Depuis la rue, en revan-
che, on a la vision d'une façade fermée et austère qui
dialogue cependant avec le milieu construit.

Planung in der Weise, dass man versuchte, eine Reihe
von miteinander und mit der Außenwelt verbundenen
Elementen zu schaffen. Durch die Anlage einer L-Form
entstand eine innere Welt, in der verschiedene Terrassen
und Räume, die zum Hof liegen, miteinander in Beziehung
stehen, so dass viele verschiedene Situationen und
räumliche Möglichkeiten in dem Haus entstehen. Die
Tatsache, dass die Innenräume auf die Außenterrassen
hin ausgerichtet sind, wird noch durch die verwendeten
Materialien in den Räumen und auf den Terrassen unterstrichen. So entstand eine innere Landschaft, die auch
mit dem allgemeinen Kontext des Viertels in Verbindung
steht. Von der Straße aus wirkt die Fassade geschlossen
und nüchtern, jedoch gut in die bebaute Umgebung
integriert.

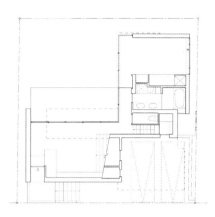

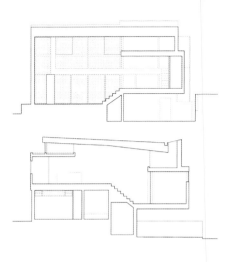

0   2   4

Ground floor

Rez-de-chaussée

Erdgeschoss

First floor

Premier étage

Erster Stock

Sections

Coupes

Schnitte

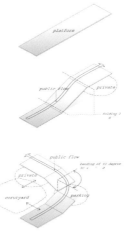

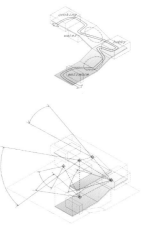

Elevations

Élévations

Aufrisse

Diagrams

Diagrammes

Schemata

1. What historical reference in particular inspires you when designing a residence?
Quelles références historiques vous inspirent en particulier lorsque vous dessinez une maison ?
Welche historische Referenz dient Ihnen als Inspiration beim Entwurf eines Hauses?

2. What is the main factor taken into consideration when designing a residence?
Quel facteur principal prenez-vous en considération lors de la conception d'une maison ?
Welche Rahmenbedingungen, bzw. Faktoren sind für Sie ausschlaggebend beim Konzipieren?

3. What room inside the home do you find most interesting to design?
Quelle pièce trouvez-vous la plus intéressante à dessiner ?
Welchen Raum des Hauses finden Sie am spannendsten zu entwerfen?

4. What is your criteria for choosing materials and finishings in a particular room?
Sur quels critères choisissez-vous les matériaux et les finitions d'une pièce ?
Welche Kriterien wenden Sie bei der Entscheidung über Materialien und Oberflächen in diesem Raum an?

1. I don't have a particular example but have some influences from historical Japanese residences and also 30's to 70's modern houses. Recently my interest moves to more 70's houses.

2. Three things in combination: Activities of the dwellers, natural environment such as light, wind and landscape, and urban context.

3. I am interested in erasing the separation of rooms and functions, trying to find flow of activities and living condition by connecting them, a house becomes more one room connected.

4. I do not choose materials which have too much strong expression, but I do rather use materials suitable to spatial compositions. Occasionally I use stronger material in order to emphasize its spatial quality. I mostly use neutral material such as white walls.

1. Je n'ai pas d'exemple particulier à donner sinon l'influence de quelques résidences japonaises historiques et de maisons modernes construites entre 1930 et 1970. Récemment, mon intérêt se focalise plutôt sur les maisons des années 1970.

2. Trois éléments combinés : les activités des occupants, l'environnement naturel (lumière, vent, paysage), et le contexte urbain.

3. Je suis plus intéressé à éliminer les séparations entre les espaces et les fonctions, et à essayer de trouver un flux d'activités et de conditions de vie grâce aux connexions entre les pièces, de manière à ce que la maison devienne une grande habitation interconnectée.

4. Je ne choisis pas des matériaux qui ont une expression trop forte, mais plutôt ceux qui conviennent aux compositions spatiales. J'emploie parfois des matériaux plus solides afin d'accentuer leur qualité spatiale. La plupart du temps, j'utilise des matériaux neutres, comme des murs blancs.

1. Ich kann niemanden im Besonderen erwähnen, aber ich bin beeinflusst von den historischen japanischen Häusern, und auch von den modernen Häusern, die zwischen den Dreißiger- und Siebzigerjahren gebaut wurden. Im Augenblick interessiere ich mich mehr für die Häuser der Siebzigerjahre.

2. Drei kombinierte Faktoren, die Aktivitäten der Bewohner, die natürliche Umgebung (Licht, Wind, Landschaft) und der städtische Kontext.

3. Ich versuche, die Trennung zwischen Räumen und Funktionen aufzuheben, und so ein Fließen der Aktivitäten und Lebensbedingungen zu erreichen, indem ich die Räume miteinander verbinde. So wird aus dem Haus ein großer, verbundener Raum.

4. Ich entscheide mich nicht für Materialien, die einen zu starken Ausdruck haben, sondern für Materialien, die sich auf besondere Art kombinieren lassen. Manchmal benutze ich starke Materialien, um eine Eigentümlichkeit des Raumes zu unterstreichen. Meist setze ich neutrale Materialien wie weiße Wände ein.

Tele-design was established with the purpose of incorporating two important tendencies of contemporary Japanese society into the vision and structure of the company. The first was the pursuit of new models of economic growth, and the second was the rapid development of telecommunications within the global economy. In this way design becomes a tool for exploration as well as a vehicle for the incorporation of the latest technologies. Tele-design consists of a multi-disciplinary team that has worked together since 1999. Its unique structure has caught the attention of clients, the press and international critics.

Tele-design a été créé avec l'objectif d'associer dans la vision et la structure de l'agence deux tendances significatives de la société japonaise contemporaine. La première est la poursuite de nouveaux modèles de croissance économique, la seconde est le développement rapide des télécommunications au sein d'une économie globale. Ainsi, la conception devient un outil d'intégration des nouvelles technologies. Tele-design se compose d'une équipe pluridisciplinaire dont les membres travaillent ensemble depuis 1999. Cette structure particulière a attiré l'attention des clients, de la presse et de la critique internationale.

Tele-design wurde gegründet, um zwei wichtige Tendenzen der heutigen japanischen Gesellschaft in die Unternehmensstruktur zu integrieren. Diese Tendenzen sind die Suche nach neuen Modellen nach dem starken Wirtschaftswachstum und die schnelle Entwicklung der Telekommunikationen in der globalen Wirtschaft. So wurde das Design zu einem Werkzeug, um die neusten Technologien zu erforschen und sich von ihnen zu nähren. Tele-design arbeitet daher seit 1999 mit ein em multidisziplinäres Team. Diese besondere Struktur erweckte viel Aufmerksamkeit seitens der Kunden und der internationalen Presse und Kritik.

ATTICS
ATTIQUES / DACHWOHNUNGEN

Phillipps / Skaife Residence

Abbot Kinney Lofts

Brooklyn Loft

Vertical Loft

House in Kuessnacht

Shoreditch Conversion

Residence in Gracia

Motoazabu Housing Complex

Rooftop

Ray 1

Bay Cities Lofts: Phase II

One of the main interests of this architect, which is seen in all his projects, is the manipulation of light as a design element. His interest is not only in illuminating spaces, but also in using the light as a medium for imprinting a specific character on each area of the project. In this case the approach is complemented by the personalities of the clients, two movie producers who are seduced by bright and strong colors. The design had to resolve two residential scenarios that could function independently within the same long and narrow, two-level unit. To make up for the lack of light in this layout, typical of New York, the architect took advantage of the fact that the unit was on the top floor of the building to create a skylight that illuminates all the central part of the residence. The existing walls on the top floor, where the living and eating areas are located, were removed to create an open space that enhances the feeling of space and light.

Phillipps / Skaife Residence

Alden Maddry Architect

New York, NY, USA, 2002
Photos © Jordi Miralles

Une des principales préoccupations de cet architecte dans sa trajectoire professionnelle est l'utilisation de la lumière comme élément de décoration. Son intérêt n'est pas seulement d'éclairer les espaces mais également d'utiliser la lumière comme média pour donner un caractère spécifique à chaque élément du projet. Cette volonté se complète ici de la personnalité de ses clients, deux producteurs de cinéma que séduisent des

Dieser Architekt hat sich während seiner ganzen Laufbahn intensiv mit dem Licht als Gestaltungselement auseinandergesetzt. Dabei geht es nicht einfach nur darum, die Räume zu beleuchten, sondern die Beleuchtung als ein Mittel zu benutzen, um jedem Bereich eines Gebäudes einen besonderen Charakter zu verleihen. Im Falle dieses Bauwerkes wird diese Vorbedingung noch durch den Charakter der Kunden ergänzt. Es handelt sich um

couleurs vives et marquées. L'architecte devait concilier deux modes de vie pour qu'ils fonctionnent indépendamment dans une même unité étroite et allongée aménagée sur deux niveaux. Pour pallier le manque de lumière de cet appartement typique de New York, l'architecte a tiré parti du fait que l'unité occupe le dernier étage de l'immeuble pour créer un puits de lumière qui illumine toute la partie centrale de l'appartement. À l'étage supérieur, le séjour et la salle à manger sont libérés de leurs cloisons et offrent un espace ouvert où s'accentue l'impression de grandeur et de luminosité.

ein Paar, das Kinofilme produziert und sich gerne von starken und glänzenden Farben verführen lässt. Durch die Gestaltung sollten zwei unabhängige Wohnbereiche innerhalb einer Einheit von zwei langen und engen Stockwerken untergebracht werden. Um den Lichtmangel auszugleichen, der normalerweise bei einer solchen, für New York typischen Gebäudeform herrscht, wurde die Tatsache ausgenutzt, dass die Räume sich im obersten Stockwerk des Gebäudes befinden und es wurde ein zentrales Dachfenster eingebaut, durch das Licht für den gesamten mittleren Teil der Wohnung fällt. Im oberen Stockwerk, wo sich die Wohn- und Speisezimmer befinden, beseitigte man alle Wände, um einen offenen, weit und hell wirkenden Raum zu schaffen.

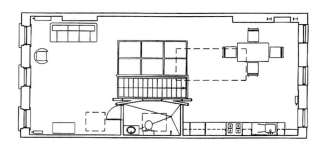

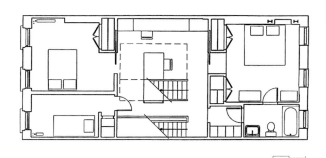

Ground floor
Rez-de-chaussée
Erdgeschoss

First floor
Premier étage
Erster Stock

0   1   2

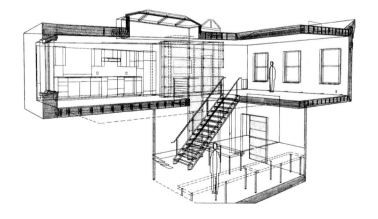

Axonometry

Axonométrie

Axonometrie

1. What historical reference in particular inspires you when designing a residence?
Quelles références historiques vous inspirent en particulier lorsque vous dessinez une maison ?
Welche historische Referenz dient Ihnen als Inspiration beim Entwurf eines Hauses?

2. What is the main factor taken into consideration when designing a residence?
Quel facteur principal prenez-vous en considération lors de la conception d'une maison ?
Welche Rahmenbedingungen, bzw. Faktoren sind für Sie ausschlaggebend beim Konzipieren?

3. What room inside the home do you find most interesting to design?
Quelle pièce trouvez-vous la plus intéressante à dessiner ?
Welchen Raum des Hauses finden Sie am spannendsten zu entwerfen?

4. What is your criteria for choosing materials and finishings in a particular room?
Sur quels critères choisissez-vous les matériaux et les finitions d'une pièce ?
Welche Kriterien wenden Sie bei der Entscheidung über Materialien und Oberflächen in diesem Raum an?

---

1. I draw inspiration from masterful individual houses and living spaces that range from the Maison de Verre in Paris to the Katsura Imperial Villa in Kyoto. But I have also drawn many ideas for my work from relatively unknown unpublished vernacular work from across the world.

2. How can I create spaces that will inspire my clients and enhance their experience of living.

3. There is not one particular room type that I find is consistently the most interesting to design. In fact the design of the interstitial spaces and connections between rooms can often be more interesting and add more to the design of the home than the composition of the individual rooms.

4. First I determine what function(s) the surface I am choosing will have. And by "function" I am not just talking about utilitarian concerns. Given these criteria, I search for a possible material that can meet these requirements.

---

1. Je tire mon inspiration de différents projets de célèbres maisons, depuis la Maison de Verre à Paris à la Villa Impériale Katsura à Kyoto. Mais j'ai également emprunté de nombreuses idées à des œuvres vernaculaires inconnues dans le monde entier.

2. Comment je peux créer des espaces qui inspireront mes clients et amélioreront leur mode de vie.

3. Il n'y a pas de type de pièce particulier que je trouve plus particulièrement intéressant à concevoir. En fait, la conception des espaces interstitiels et des connexions entre les pièces peut souvent être plus intéressante et ajouter plus dans la conception de la maison que la composition de pièces individuelles.

4. Tout d'abord, je détermine quelle(s) fonction(s), et pas seulement en termes d'utilité, doit avoir la surface que je choisis. Et c'est une fois ce critère défini que je recherche les matériaux qui peuvent satisfaire à ces besoins.

---

1. Mich inspirieren verschiedene Beispiele berühmter Planungen für Wohnhäuser, angefangen bei dem Maison de Verre in Paris bis zur Kaiserstadt Katsura in Kyoto. Ich habe aber auch viele Ideen in meinen Arbeiten umgesetzt, die aus volkstümlichen architektonischen Werken stammen und die weltweit relativ unbekannt sind und selten veröffentlicht wurden.

2. Wie kann ich Räume schaffen, die meine Kunden inspirieren und ihre Erfahrung im Wohnen betonen.

3. Es gibt keinen besonderen Typ Raum, den ich interessanter als andere finde. Tatsächlich kann die Gestaltung von Zwischenräumen und Verbindungen zwischen den verschiedenen Zimmern interessanter sein und mehr zum Design eines Hauses beitragen als die Gestaltung der individuellen Räume.

4. Zunächst bestimme ich die Funktion, nicht nur im Bezug auf die Benutzung, und sie wird die Fläche einnehmen, die ich wähle. Nachdem dieses Kriterium definiert wurde, wähle ich die möglichen Materialien für diese Bestimmung.

Alden Maddry Architect was founded in the spring of 1996. The firm specializes in cultural and residential designs, and projects related to art, in New York City and the surrounding area. Maddry is especially interested in the construction details and depends on the talent of expert workers and artisans of the region to carry out their projects. They have used alternative energy sources — solar and geothermal — in many of their past projects.

L'agence Alden Maddry Architect, créée au printemps 1996, est spécialisée dans la conception de bâtiments culturels et résidentiels et de projets liés à l'art, à New York et ses environs. Maddry s'intéresse particulièrement aux détails de construction et s'appuie sur des ouvriers et artisans qualifiés et talentueux de la région pour réaliser ses projets. L'agence a utilisé des sources d'énergie alternatives — solaire et géothermie — dans nombre de ses précédents projets.

Alden Maddry Architect wurde im Frühjahr 1996 gegründet. Das Unternehmen hat sich auf Projekte in den Bereichen Kunst, Kultur und Stadtwohnungen in New York und Umgebung spezialisiert. Bei Maddry interessiert man sich besonders für die Bauprozesse; und die Arbeiten werden in Zusammenarbeit mit begabten Arbeitern und Handwerkern aus der Region durchgeführt. In vielen, bereits von Maddry errichteten Gebäuden wurden alternative Energiequellen wie Solarenergie oder Erdwärme benutzt.

The Abbot Kinney neighborhood in Venice, California, is rapidly becoming an artist's district. A growing number of designers, multimedia firms, and artists choose this neighborhood, which is turning into a lively and diverse community. These professionals are not only looking for a section of the city that identifies with their way of life, but also for interior spaces that adapt to their requirements. They are searching for more casual, informal, and flexible environments that allow them to live and work in the same space. This project con-sists of a typical adaptation of the traditional artist's loft, with large, open spaces that can be used for living or working, as required. The plan includes three different adjacent lofts that share the same structure, materials, and color palette, giving it the appearance of a compact building. These characteristics allow the creation of a continuous façade and a commercial row facing the street. All the units are separated by patios and are equipped with balconies, terraces, and glassed-in areas.

Abbot Kinney Lofts

Mark Mack Architects

Venice, CA, USA, 2001
Photos © Undine Pröhl

Le quartier d'Abbot Kinney, à Venice (Californie), est rapidement devenu un quartier d'artistes. Chaque année, un nombre croissant de designers, d'entreprises du multimédia et d'artistes choisit de s'y installer et y forme une communauté vivante et diversifiée. Ils y cherchent – et y trouvent – non seulement un quartier identifiable à leur mode de vie mais également des espaces intérieurs adaptés à leurs besoins. Les princi-

Abbot Kinney in Venice, Kalifornien, entwickelt sich zur Zeit zunehmend zu einem Künstlerviertel. Jedes Jahr gibt es mehr Designer, Multimedia-Unternehmen und Künstler, die sich dieses Viertel für ihre Studios aussuchen, wodurch eine vielseitige und lebendige Gemeinschaft entstanden ist. Diese Menschen in kreativen Berufen suchen nicht nur ein Viertel in der Stadt, das ihrem Lebensstil zusagt, sondern auch Räume, die ihren Bedürfnissen ent-

pales caractéristiques de cette quête sont de bénéficier d'un environnement plus décontracté, plus informel et plus souple qui permette de vivre et de travailler à l'intérieur d'un même espace. Ce projet est une adaptation typologique du loft d'artiste traditionnel en ce qu'il crée des espaces vastes et ouverts exploitables, selon les besoins, aussi bien pour vivre que pour travailler. Le bâtiment est compartimenté en trois lofts différents et adjacents, qui partagent des matériaux et des palettes de couleurs identiques de sorte qu'on ait une impression d'unité. Cela permet d'offrir une façade continue avec une galerie commerciale sur la rue, chacun des volumes, avec baies vitrées, balcons et terrasses, étant séparé par des patios.

sprechen. Weniger strenge, flexible und moderne Räume, in denen man gleichzeitig leben und arbeiten kann, werden besonders gesucht. Dieses Projekt besteht in einer typischen Gestaltung eines traditionellen Künstler-Loftes, in dem weite und offene Räume geschaffen werden, die man sowohl zum Wohnen als auch zum Arbeiten benutzen kann. Das Gebäude beherbergt drei benachbarte Lofts, die die gleiche Struktur, Materialien und Farbpalette teilen, so dass ein zusammenhängendes Ganzes entsteht. So konnte auch eine durchgehende Fassade und ein kommerziell genutzter Weg zur Straße hin geschaffen werden, während alle Lofts durch Höfe getrennt sind und ihre eigenen verglasten Bereiche, Balkone und Terrassen haben.

Ground floor
Rez-de-chaussée
Erdgeschoss

First floor
Premier étage
Erster Stock

Second floor
Deuxième étage
Zweiter Stock

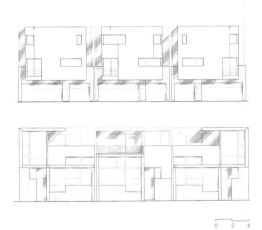

Elevations

Élévations

Aufrisse

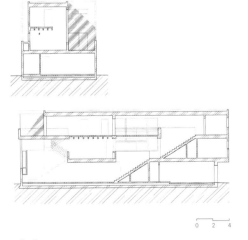

Sections

Coupes

Schnitte

Mark Mack, along with his former partner Andrew Batey, earned his reputation as an architect in California mainly for his single-family home and villa designs in the early 1980's. He established his own office in San Francisco in 1984 and then moved to Venice, California in 1993. His approach to design is influenced by his academic work and restless curiosity. He was a professor in the School of Architecture at the University of California, Los Angeles. He was also a cofounder of Archetype Magazine and has contributed numerous articles to different magazines.

Mark Mack, avec son ancien associé Andrew Batey, a forgé sa réputation d'architecte en Californie principalement grâce à ses maisons et à ses villas au début des années 1980. Il a créé sa propre agence à San Francisco en 1984 puis est parti s'installer à Venice en 1993. Son approche du design est influencée par son œuvre académique et sa curiosité insatiable. Il a été professeur à l'école d'architecture de l'université de Californie à Los Angeles. Également cofondateur d'*Archetype Magazine*, il a publié de nombreux articles dans plusieurs publications.

Mark Mack begann seine Karriere Anfang der Achtzigerjahre mit der Planung von Einfamilienhäusern und Villen in Kalifornien zusammen mit seinem ehemaligen Teilhaber Andrew Batey. 1984 gründete er in San Francisco sein eigenes Unternehmen, das er 1993 nach Venice, Kalifornien, verlegte. Seine Interessen und seine akademische Arbeit beeinflussen seinen Gestaltungsstil. Er war Professor am Fachbereich Architektur der Universität von Kalifornien in Los Angeles. Ebenso war er Mitbegründer der Zeitschrift Archetype Magazine, in der er zahlreiche Artikel veröffentlicht hat.

This project is located in a space that was originally occupied by a lighting factory in an industrial neighborhood of the borough of Brooklyn, New York. The project had to fulfill the expectations of the clients, two artists from Brazil who wanted a loft-style space that would provide various settings for living as well as for working. A translucent, retractable wall defines the different areas in the lower level and adds character to the space. The natural light from a skylight flows through the translucent wall to illuminate the interior of the loft's living area. A dramatic metal stairway, light and equally transparent, connects the lower level with the top level where the bedrooms and an outdoor terrace are found. At the same time the stairway serves as an esthetic reference to the industrial nature of the building's past. The original façade, consisting of a garage door, and the new aluminum and wood features emphasize the contrast between the warm and organic interior and the heavy and metallic materials of the exterior.

Brooklyn Loft

Basil Walter Architects

New York, NY, USA, 2002
Photos © Bilyana Dimitrova

Ce bâtiment occupe un terrain du quartier industriel de Brooklyn, à New York, autrefois occupé par une usine d'éclairage. Le projet devait satisfaire les attentes des clients, un couple d'artistes brésiliens qui voulaient disposer d'un espace de type loft où ils pourraient aussi bien vivre que travailler. Une cloison rétractable et translucide définit et attribue leur fonction aux différents espaces de l'étage inférieur. La lumière naturelle

Dieses Gebäude befindet sich auf einem Grundstück im Industrieviertel von Brooklyn, New York, auf dem einst eine Lampenfabrik stand. Die Kunden, ein brasilianisches Künstlerpaar, wünschten sich eine Art Loft, in dem man sowohl wohnen als auch arbeiten kann. Eine einziehbare und lichtdurchlässige Wand definiert und bereichert die verschiedenen Zonen im Erdgeschoss. Das Tageslicht dringt über ein Dachfenster ein und filtert sich durch die

en provenance du puits de lumière est filtrée par la cloison translucide et éclaire l'intérieur de la pièce de séjour. Un escalier métallique, théâtral, léger et transparent, relie l'étage au niveau supérieur où se trouvent les chambres et une terrasse extérieure. L'escalier est également un souvenir esthétique de l'ancienne nature industrielle de l'édifice. La façade originelle, signalée par une porte de garage, et la nouvelle terrasse en aluminium et bois accentuent le contraste entre l'intérieur chaleureux et organique et les détails métalliques et pesants de l'extérieur.

lichtdurchlässige Wand, so dass auch das Innere des Wohnbereiches beleuchtet wird. Eine dramatisch wirkende, leichte und ebenfalls transparente Metalltreppe verbindet das Erdgeschoss mit dem Obergeschoss, in dem sich die Schlafzimmer und die Terrasse im Freien befinden. Die Treppe dient auch als ästhetische Anspielung auf die industrielle Vergangenheit des Gebäudes. Die Originalfassade, die aus einer Garagentür besteht, und die neue Terrasse aus Aluminium und Holz unterstreichen den deutlich erkennbaren Unterschied zwischen den warm und organisch wirkenden Materialien im Inneren und den schweren Details aus Metall außen.

1. What historical reference in particular inspires you when designing a residence?
   Quelles références historiques vous inspirent en particulier lorsque vous dessinez une maison ?
   Welche historische Referenz dient Ihnen als Inspiration beim Entwurf eines Hauses?

2. What is the main factor taken into consideration when designing a residence?
   Quel facteur principal prenez-vous en considération lors de la conception d'une maison ?
   Welche Rahmenbedingungen, bzw. Faktoren sind für Sie ausschlaggebend beim Konzipieren?

3. What room inside the home do you find most interesting to design?
   Quelle pièce trouvez-vous la plus intéressante à dessiner ?
   Welchen Raum des Hauses finden Sie am spannendsten zu entwerfen?

4. What is your criteria for choosing materials and finishings in a particular room?
   Sur quels critères choisissez-vous les matériaux et les finitions d'une pièce ?
   Welche Kriterien wenden Sie bei der Entscheidung über Materialien und Oberflächen in diesem Raum an?

1. It is the reference to historical methods rather than any direct period references which find their way most consistently into our work. A study of historical systems of design and construction creates a process that integrates time tested methods with free-thinking inventiveness.

2. What is most important is keeping the brightest torch shining firmly on those qualities of the house that make it beautiful, functional and economical and not getting sidetracked during the process. This requires continual reserves of energy and patience.

3. It is the connections between the various rooms or spaces in a home that pose the most challenging design issues.

4. The space itself must be the dominant image. Instances of local color or pattern must complement the effect of the space itself, and not the other way around.

1. Dans notre travail, nous faisons généralement référence à des méthodes plus qu'à des périodes historiques. L'étude des systèmes historiques de conception et de construction est un processus qui intègre des méthodes éprouvées dans une inventivité libérée.

2. Il est plus important de mettre en valeur les qualités qui font qu'une maison est belle, fonctionnelle et économique, sans s'en écarter pendant le processus. Cela requiert des réserves continuelles d'énergie et de patience.

3. Les connexions entre les différentes pièces ou espaces présentent le défi le plus important au cours de la conception.

4. L'espace en soi doit être l'image dominante. Les éléments ponctuels de couleur ou de forme doivent venir compléter l'effet d'espace, et non l'inverse.

1. Bei unserer Arbeit benutzen wir normalerweise eher Referenzen auf historische Methoden als auf konkrete Epochen der Zeitgeschichte. Eine Studie der historischen Systeme bei der Gestaltung und beim Bau stellt einen Prozess dar, der erprobte Methoden in eine skeptische Erfindungsgabe integriert.

2. Es ist wichtig, die Eigenschaften zu betonen, die dafür sorgen, dass ein Haus oder eine Wohnung schön, funktionell und ökonomisch werden. Diese Eigenschaften darf man während des Gesamtprozesses nicht vergessen, und dazu braucht man ständige Energie und Geduldsreserven.

3. Die Elemente, die die größte Herausforderung beim Planungsprozess darstellen, sind die Verbindungen zwischen den verschiedenen Räumen und Bereichen.

4. Der Raum selbst sollte das dominierende Bild sein. Einzelne, farbige Elemente oder Formen sollten die Wirkung des Raumes ergänzen, und nicht umgekehrt.

Basil Walter Architects was officially launched in 2001 after practicing for twelve years as Sweeny Walter Architects, founded in 1998. Today it is an organization of 13 architects and designers led by Basil Walter and his associate Brenda Bello. Basil Walter Architects and his previous firm were responsible for a variety of projects ranging from private residences to design offices and event planning. The firm, based in New York City, has ample experience in designing emblematic buildings as well as in renovating the interiors of many apartments in historic buildings.

L'agence Basil Walter Architects a été officiellement créée en 2001 après avoir fonctionné pendant douze ans sous le nom de Sweeny Walter Architects, fondée en 1998. Elle comprend 13 architectes et designers dirigés par Basil Walter et son associée Brenda Bello. Basil Walter Architects, et l'agence antérieure, ont été responsables de nombreux projets allant des résidences privées à des bureaux de design et à l'organisation d'événements. L'agence, basée à New York, a une grande expérience dans la conception d'immeubles emblématiques ainsi que dans la rénovation d'appartements situés dans des buildings historiques.

Basil Walter Architects wurde offiziell 2001 gegründet, nachdem bereits 12 Jahre unter dem Namen Sweeny Walter Architects, gegründet 1989, gearbeitet wurde. Heute arbeiten 13 freie Architekten und Innenarchitekten für Basil Walter und seine Gesellschafterin Brenda Bello. Basil Walter Architects und die Vorgängerfirma haben bereits sehr verschiedene Planungen durchgeführt, Privatwohnungen, edle Büroräume und Bauten für Veranstaltungen. In New York blickt man auf eine lange Erfahrung in der Planung von emblematischen Gebäuden und Innenrenovierung von Wohnungen in historischen Gebäuden zurück.

This project is located in an old industrial space in the 11th District in Paris. It is not a typical industrial building with a horizontal, open, and fluid space, but one that is vertical and sturdy, made of wood and metal covered with rustic walls of exposed brick. The interior was opened up by removing all the dividing walls to create a naturally illuminated space of generous proportions. The structural and architectural elements that define and create the character of the interior space were preserved. The vertical aspect of the building offered the opportunity to create a design that exceeded the limits of a traditional loft. The project attempted to create a vertical sequence that highlight the dynamism of the design. Making an analogy to a movie script, the design lays out a sequence between what is seen, what is not seen, and what one hopes to see, all integrated into a common setting. The building was left completely intact, and certain aspects of the design took the form of solid spaces with opaque and translucent qualities. These volumes become anecdotes within the sequence.

Vertical Loft

Insite Architecture Design

Paris, France, 2003
Photos © Georges Fessy

Situé sur un ancien terrain industriel du XIᵉ arrondissement de Paris, ce bâtiment industriel ne montre pas la typologie habituelle, horizontale, ouverte et fluide, mais celle d'un petit immeuble vertical à solide charpente de bois et de métal enveloppée dans des murs rustiques en briques apparentes. L'intérieur a été ouvert en supprimant toutes les cloisons intérieures pour créer un espace de généreuses proportions éclairé naturel-

Dieses Loft befindet sich in einem ehemaligen Industriegebäude im 11. Arrondissement von Paris. Es handelt sich nicht um das typische Fabrikgebäude mit einem horizontalen, offenen und fließenden Aufbau, sondern um eine robuste Struktur aus Holz und Metall, die sich vertikal aufbaut und von einer rustikalen Wand aus unverputztem Ziegelstein umgeben ist. Die Innenräume wurden erweitert, indem man alle Zwischenwände abriss. So

lement. Les éléments structurels et architecturaux qui définissent et créent le caractère du volume intérieur ont été préservés. La verticalité de ce volume offrait l'opportunité de concevoir un projet allant au-delà des limites du loft traditionnel en créant une séquence verticale qui révélerait le dynamisme du programme. Par analogie avec un scénario de film, le décor définit une séquence entre ce qui se voit, ce qui ne se voit pas et ce qu'on espère voir, dans un même espace. Le bâtiment ayant été laissé totalement intact, il en reste des pièces solides, jouant sur l'opacité et le translucide, dont les volumes sont des anecdotes à l'intérieur de la séquence.

erreichte man großzügige Proportionen und ließ das Tageslicht in die Räume eindringen. Die strukturellen und architektonischen Elemente, die die Räume prägen, wurden beibehalten und wieder hergestellt. Die vertikale Gliederung des Gebäudes machte es möglich, Räumlichkeiten zu schaffen, in denen mehr Kreativität als in einer traditionellen Fabriketage möglich war. Es wurde eine vertikale Sequenz geschaffen, die die Dynamik der Planung zeigte. Analog zu dem Drehbuch eines Films wird mit der Gestaltung eine Sequenz vorgeschlagen, eine Sequenz zwischen dem, was man sieht, dem was man nicht sieht und dem, was man zu sehen erwartet, all das am gleichen Schauplatz. Die Formen wurden absolut respektiert und bestimmte Aspekte der Gestaltung zeigten sich in festen Elementen, die doch lichtdurchlässig oder opak sind. Diese Formen werden zu Anekdoten innerhalb einer Sequenz.

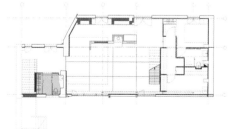

Ground floor
Rez-de-chaussée
Erdgeschoss

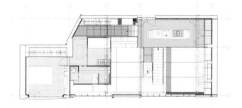

First floor
Premier étage
Erster Stock

Second floor
Deuxième étage
Zweiter Stock

0   2   4

La base structurelle de ce projet, qui abrite désormais trois appartements de luxe dans le quartier d'Islington, au nord-ouest de Londres, est un bâtiment abandonné depuis plus de dix ans. Une des originalités de ce projet est que chaque unité a été conçue individuellement pour pouvoir obtenir une atmosphère propre par la lumière, la couleur et la disposition de l'espace. Une attention particulière a été portée à l'aspect pratique

Ein seit über zehn Jahren leer stehendes Gebäude war Gegenstand dieser Planung eines Wohnhauses, in dem drei Luxuswohnungen untergebracht sind. Es liegt im Nordosten Londons im Viertel Islington. Was dieses Gebäude sehr originell macht, ist die Tatsache, dass jede der Wohnungen individuell geplant wurde, um in jeder mithilfe des Lichtes, der Farben und der Anordnung der Räume eine eigene Atmosphäre zu schaffen. Besondere

avec de grands espaces de rangement, un éclairage intelligent, des sonorisations, et des salles de bains et cuisines dotées des dernières innovations technologiques. Les appartements des étages inférieurs occupent un seul niveau tandis que le dernier niveau est rendu spectaculaire par sa double hauteur. Une grande verrière en verre et acier couvre l'espace et encadre le panorama depuis la salle de séjour. Les matériaux et les détails intérieurs, où prédominent l'acier inoxydable, le bois et le verre, accentuent le caractère de cet espace.

Aufmerksamkeit wurde beim Entwurf auf die praktische Umgebung der Wohnung gerichtet. So gibt es geräumige Aufbewahrungsbereiche, eine intelligente Beleuchtung, Tonsysteme, Bäder und Küchen, die mit den letzten technischen Neuheiten ausgestattet sind. Die Wohnungen der unteren Stockwerke liegen auf einer Etage, während die im letzten Stockwerk zweistöckig und besonders schön ist. Eine große Markise aus Stahl und Kristall umfasst die doppelte Höhe des Raumes und bildet einen Rahmen für das Wohnzimmer dieser Wohnung. Die Materialien und Elemente im Inneren, bei denen Edelstahl, Holz und Glas dominieren, unterstreichen noch die Wirkung der Räume.

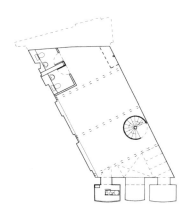
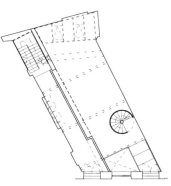
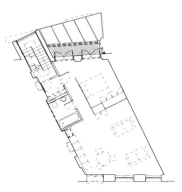
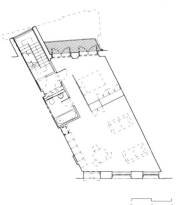

0   2   4

Basement plan

Sous-sol

Untergeschoss

Ground floor

Rez-de-chaussée

Erdgeschoss

First floor

Premier étage

Erster Stock

Second floor

Deuxième étage

Zweiter Stock

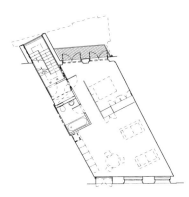

Third floor

Troisième étage

Dritter Stock

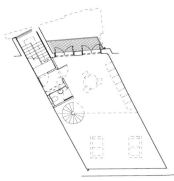

Fourth floor

Quatrième étage

Vierter Stock

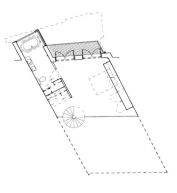

Fifth floor

Cinquième étage

Fünfter Stock

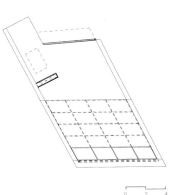

Roof plan

Plan de toiture

Dachgrundriss

0   2   4

1. What historical reference in particular inspires you when designing a residence?
Quelles références historiques vous inspirent en particulier lorsque vous dessinez une maison ?
Welche historische Referenz dient Ihnen als Inspiration beim Entwurf eines Hauses?

2. What is the main factor taken into consideration when designing a residence?
Quel facteur principal prenez-vous en considération lors de la conception d'une maison ?
Welche Rahmenbedingungen, bzw. Faktoren sind für Sie ausschlaggebend beim Konzipieren?

3. What room inside the home do you find most interesting to design?
Quelle pièce trouvez-vous la plus intéressante à dessiner ?
Welchen Raum des Hauses finden Sie am spannendsten zu entwerfen?

4. What is your criteria for choosing materials and finishings in a particular room?
Sur quels critères choisissez-vous les matériaux et les finitions d'une pièce ?
Welche Kriterien wenden Sie bei der Entscheidung über Materialien und Oberflächen in diesem Raum an?

1. A house should be a sanctuary and a place that works for the owners; thus for me it is a combination of a temple, a machine for living in and the best most luxurious hotel.

2. It is a question of meeting the needs of the client, making the spaces work for their lifestyle and creating elegance. We also look to create wonderful spaces that make the most of the features of the site or building.

3. The living room and kitchen have to allow for many functions to occur. They are used throughout the day in various ways. These spaces are a fascinating challenge to create elegance, comfort and function.

4. Beauty, practicality, longevity.

1. Une maison doit être un sanctuaire et un lieu pratique pour ses occupants ; aussi est-ce pour moi à la fois un temple, une machine pour vivre et le plus luxueux des hôtels.

2. Il faut satisfaire les besoins du client, faire en sorte que les espaces fonctionnent suivant son mode de vie et créer de l'élégance. Nous cherchons également à créer des espaces merveilleux qui profitent le plus possible du site ou du bâtiment.

3. La salle de séjour et la cuisine doivent assurer de nombreuses fonctions, utilisées de différentes manières pendant la journée. Ces espaces sont particulièrement fascinants au moment de créer des ambiances élégantes, confortables et fonctionnelles.

4. Beauté, praticité et longévité.

1. Ein Haus sollte eine Art heiliger Ort, aber auch ein praktischer Ort für die Besitzer sein. Deshalb ist es eine Kombination aus Tempel, Wohnapparat und Luxushotel.

2. Man muss die Bedürfnisse des Kunden kennen, und nützliche Räume für seinen Lebensstil und gleichzeitig Eleganz schaffen. Wir versuchen auch wundervolle Räume zu gestalten, mit denen wir die Möglichkeiten des Grundstückes oder des Hauses voll ausschöpfen. Vielleicht große Fenster, um den Ausblick zu genießen oder Räume doppelter Höhe, die die wichtigen Aspekte des Gebäudes miteinander verbinden.

3. Das Wohnzimmer und die Küche müssen vielen Funktionen dienen, da sie im Laufe des Tages auf verschiedene Weise genutzt werden. Diese Räume sind besonders interessant bei der Gestaltung eleganter, komfortabler und funktioneller Wohnatmosphären.

4. Schönheit, Funktionalität und Dauerhaftigkeit.

Gregory Phillips Architects is a young firm based in London. It consists of Gregory Phillips, who worked with David Chipperfield, and two other architects — Jay Salero, who practiced at Foster and Partners for three years, and Cathy Curran, a collaborator of Richard Rogers for four years — who act as project directors. Phillips, who founded his own office in 1991, is a devotee of esthetics and modern technology, and of developing any project of any scale.

Gregory Phillips Architects est une jeune agence basée à Londres. Elle se compose de Gregory Phillips, qui a travaillé avec David Chipperfield, et de deux autres architectes – Jay Salero, qui a travaillé trois ans chez Foster and Partners, et Cathy Curran, collaboratrice de Richard Rogers pendant quatre ans – qui ont le rôle de directeurs de projet. Phillips, qui a créé sa propre agence en 1991, est un passionné d'esthétique et de technologie moderne, et avide de création quels que soient le projet et l'échelle.

Gregory Phillips Architects ist ein junges Architekturbüro mit Sitz in London. Hier arbeiten Gregory Phillips selbst, der auch mit David Chipperfield kollaboriert hatte, und weitere Architekten, die verschiedene Projektleitungen übernehmen, nämlich Jay Salero, der drei Jahre lang bei Foster and Partners arbeitete, und Cathy Curran, die vier Jahre mit Richard Rogers zusammenarbeitete. Phillips, der sein Unternehmen 1991 gründete, liebt die Ästhetik und moderne Technologie und er sieht es als eine Herausforderung an, jegliches Projekt jeder Größenordnung zu übernehmen.

This residential project in Barcelona consisted of renovating the upper level of an old industrial building with a pitched roof. The original space had a large ground floor and a small top floor with access to a terrace. The primary objectives were to flood the space with natural light and to create spacious rooms. A large skylight was installed over the living and dining areas while other smaller openings were made to illuminate the bathrooms. The framework crossing the grand central skylight causes the light to reflect in several directions, creating a changing environment throughout the day. The layout of the space is organized around a furniture element that separates the night area from the day area. It does not reach as far as the ceiling or to the outside walls of the apartment, a feature that emphasizes the fluidity of the space. The piece serves as a shelf on the social side and as a closet on the private side. The communication between the sleeping area and the salon, or between the salon and the kitchen, is more flexible and striking because of the sliding doors.

Residence in Gracia

Sandra Aparicio + Forteza Carbonell Associats

Barcelona, Spain, 2002
Photos © Santiago Garcès

Ce projet d'habitation consistait en la rénovation de l'étage d'attique, avec une couverture à deux pentes, d'un ancien édifice industriel de Barcelone. Le volume originel offrait une grande surface au sol au rez-de-chaussée et un petit étage donnant accès à une terrasse. L'objectif principal était d'inonder l'espace de lumière naturelle et de créer des pièces plus grandes. Pour ce faire, on a créé une grande verrière au-dessus

Diese Wohnung entstand durch die Renovierung eines Penthouses mit Satteldach in einem alten Industriegebäude in Barcelona. Die Originalräume besaßen ein geräumiges Erdgeschoss und ein kleines Obergeschoss mit Zugang zur Terrasse. Vor allem wollte man viel Tageslicht in die Räume bringen und sie weitläufig wirken lassen. Dazu wurde ein großes Dachfenster eingebaut, das zu einem prägenden Element im Wohnzimmer und

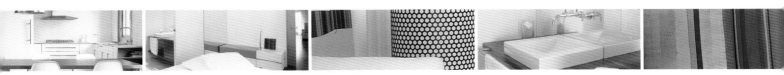

des salles de séjour et à manger tandis que des ouvertures plus petites étaient aménagées pour la salle de bains. Les éléments croisant la grande verrière centrale font se refléter la lumière dans plusieurs directions et créent ainsi une atmosphère changeante tout au long de la journée. L'espace s'organise à partir d'un meuble central, qui sépare la zone diurne de la zone nocturne sans toucher ni le plafond ni les murs de manière à accentuer la fluidité de l'espace. Il joue le rôle de bibliothèque dans la zone sociale et de placard dans la partie privée. La relation entre la chambre et le salon ou entre le salon et la cuisine est plus souple et plus marquée grâce aux portes coulissantes.

Esszimmer wurde. Die Helligkeit dringt durch kleinere Fenster in die Bäder ein. Die Schnittstellen, die sich durch das große zentrale Dachfenster ziehen, verursachen verschiedene Lichtreflexe, die die Stimmung in den Räumen im Laufe des Tages sehr verändern. Der Raum organisiert sich um ein zentrales Möbelstück herum, das die Bereiche für den Tag und die Nacht trennt und weder die Decke noch die Wände der Wohnung berührt, so dass der Raum sehr fließend wirkt. Zum Wohnbereich hin dient dieses Möbel als Regal, zu den Schlafzimmern hin als Schrank. Die Beziehung zwischen den Schlafzimmern und dem Wohnzimmern und zwischen dem Wohnzimmer und der Küche wird durch Schiebetüren noch flexibler und fließender.

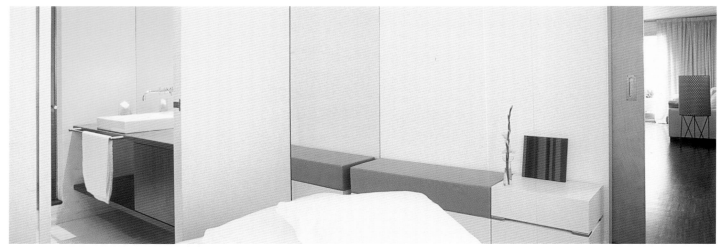

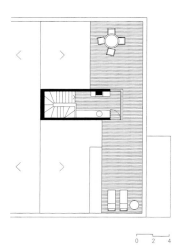

Plan
Plan
Grundriss

Roof plan
Plan de toiture
Dachgrundriss

0   2   4

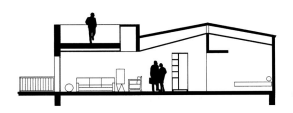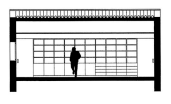

0　1　2

Sections
Coupes
Schnitte

1. What historical reference in particular inspires you when designing a residence?
Quelles références historiques vous inspirent en particulier lorsque vous dessinez une maison ?
Welche historische Referenz dient Ihnen als Inspiration beim Entwurf eines Hauses?

2. What is the main factor taken into consideration when designing a residence?
Quel facteur principal prenez-vous en considération lors de la conception d'une maison ?
Welche Rahmenbedingungen, bzw. Faktoren sind für Sie ausschlaggebend beim Konzipieren?

3. What room inside the home do you find most interesting to design?
Quelle pièce trouvez-vous la plus intéressante à dessiner ?
Welchen Raum des Hauses finden Sie am spannendsten zu entwerfen?

4. What is your criteria for choosing materials and finishings in a particular room?
Sur quels critères choisissez-vous les matériaux et les finitions d'une pièce ?
Welche Kriterien wenden Sie bei der Entscheidung über Materialien und Oberflächen in diesem Raum an?

1. We find inspiration in different historical periods, probably because our projects are more related to interior design.

2. Fulfilling the functional requirements and the location of the project.

3. The living room is where people spend most of their time, so it is probably there that the overall feeling of the house can be summed up.

4. We usually choose three or four materials that are carried through all the rooms in the house. They always tend to be high quality materials.

1. Nous trouvons notre inspiration dans les différentes périodes historiques, probablement parce que nos projets sont plus liés à la décoration intérieure.

2. La satisfaction des exigences fonctionnelles et l'emplacement du projet.

3. La salle de séjour est l'endroit où les gens passent le plus clair de leur temps, aussi est-ce probablement là que se synthétise l'atmosphère générale de la maison.

4. Nous choisissons habituellement trois ou quatre matériaux que nous reprenons dans toutes les pièces de la maison. Il s'agit généralement de matériaux nobles.

1. Vielleicht finden wir deshalb zu verschiedenen Zeitpunkten der Geschichte Referenzen, weil unsere Projekte sich mehr mit der Innenarchitektur beschäftigen.

2. Das notwendige Wohnprogramm und der Standort.

3. Das Wohnzimmer ist der Ort, in dem man sich meistens mehr Stunden aufzuhalten pflegt, und in dem man die allgemeine Atmosphäre des Hauses oder der Wohnung zusammenfassen kann.

4. Normalerweise entscheiden wir uns für drei oder vier Materialien und wiederholen diese in allen Räumen der Wohnung. Wir arbeiten meist mit edlen Materialien.

Ignacio Forteza of Forteza Carbonell Associats, and Sandra Aparicio have collaborated on interior design projects since 1995. Forteza Carbonell Associats also does architectural design. Their work is based on respect and function, interpreting the needs of the client and trying to impart a magical sense to the spaces that will provoke thinking. The use of materials in their original form, and a careful execution of the construction is characteristic of their work.

Ignacio Forteza, de Forteza Carbonell Associats, et Sandra Aparicio collaborent sur des projets de décoration intérieure depuis 1995. Forteza Carbonell Associats s'occupe également de conception architecturale. Leur travail se fonde sur le respect et la fonction, interprétant les besoins du client et essayant de donner aux espaces un sens magique qui provoquera la réflexion. L'emploi de matériaux sous leur forme originelle et l'exécution soigneuse de la construction sont caractéristiques de leur travail.

Ignacio Forteza von Forteza Carbonell Associats und Sandra Aparicio arbeiten schon seit 1995 bei der Gestaltung von Innenräumen zusammen. Forteza Carbonell Associats beschäftigt sich auch mit Architektur. Die Arbeitsphilosophie dieser Architekten stützt sich auf die Pfeiler Respekt und Funktionalität. Sie interpretieren die Bedürfnisse ihrer Kunden und versuchen die Räume magisch und suggestiv zu gestalten. Typisch für ihre Planungen ist die Verwendung von Materialien in ihrem ursprünglichen Zustand und eine sehr sorgfältiges Arbeiten beim Bau.

This project consisted of a total renovation to convert an old 1980's building, used as a photography studio, into a residential complex. Although the building had no special architectural character, it did have a double structure that created different kinds of spaces in its interior. Some rooms had very high ceilings while others were of a conventional height. After removing the walls these variations resulted in areas with different floor and ceiling heights, which created an interesting layout. The architects always begin with the premise that a conversion not only means changing the use of a building, but also adapting it to create a new kind of space. In this sense they visualized the possibility of excavating and creating a patio around the ground floor, making it easier to use. This way they not only adapted the interior space, but the exterior experienced a dramatic transformation as well. During the renovation's design process, the architects tried to employ the same methods that are normally used for new construction. This entailed the careful analysis of the location's characteristics and an attempt at maximizing the use of the building through intelligent design.

Motoazabu Housing Complex

Yasushi Ikeda, Akiko Kokubun / IKDS

Minatoku, Tokyo, Japan, 2003
Photos © Toshiharu Kitajima

L'objectif de ce projet consistait en la rénovation complète d'un ancien édifice des années 1980, utilisé comme studio de photographie, et de le convertir en un ensemble résidentiel. Bien que le bâtiment n'ait aucun caractère architectural particulier, il présentait une double structure qui créait à l'intérieur différents types d'espaces. Certaines pièces montraient de très hauts plafonds tandis que d'autres avaient une hauteur conven-

Hier wurde der gesamte Umbau eines ehemaligen Fotostudios aus den Achtzigerjahren in einen Wohnungs-komplex geplant. Obwohl das Gebäude keine spezifischen, architektonischen Kennzeichen aufwies, gab es dennoch eine doppelte Struktur, durch die verschiedene Raumtypen im Inneren entstanden. Es gab besonders hohe und normal hohe Räume. Nach dem Abriss der Wände entstanden also Räumlichkeiten, in denen die

tionnelle. Après avoir supprimé les séparations, ces disparités offrirent des pièces de différentes hauteurs de plafond, produisant un intéressant jeu intérieur. Les architectes partent toujours de l'idée qu'une conversion ne signifie pas seulement modifier la destination d'un bâtiment mais aussi l'adapter pour créer un nouveau type d'espace. Ils ont ainsi vu la possibilité de creuser et de créer un patio autour du sous-sol pour le rendre plus accessible. De cette manière, ils n'adaptent pas seulement l'espace intérieur mais transforment également l'extérieur de façon dramatique. Dans le processus de conception de la rénovation, les architectes ont essayé d'employer les mêmes méthodes que celles utilisées pour une construction neuve, c'est-à-dire d'analyser en détail les caractéristiques du lieu et de maximiser l'emploi de l'édifice par une conception intelligente.

Böden oder die Decken verschiedene Höhen hatten, was eine interessante Wirkung erzielte. Die Architekten gingen davon aus, dass man durch einen Umbau nicht nur die Nutzungsart eines Gebäudes verändert, sondern dass man eine neue Wohnlandschaft schafft. So kamen sie zum Beispiel auf die Idee, einen Hof um das Erd-geschoss anzulegen, damit man dieses besser ausnutzen konnte. Also wurde nicht nur das Innere umgebaut, sondern auch von außen wurden große Veränderungen vorgenommen. Bei der Umgestaltung des Gebäudes versuchte man die gleiche Methode zu benutzen, die normalerweise bei einem Neubau angewendet wird. Man analysierte also die Eigenschaften des Bauplatzes genau und versuchte, dem Gebäude durch intelligente Ge-staltung eine größtmögliche Nutzbarkeit zu geben.

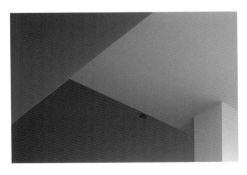 

0 2 4

Basement

Sous-sol

Untergeschoss

Ground floor

Rez-de-chaussée

Erdgeschoss

First floor

Premier étage

Erster Stock

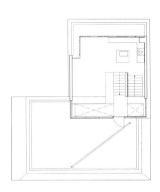

Second floor

Deuxième étage

Zweiter Stock

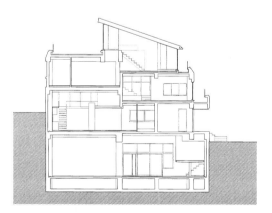

Section

Coupe

Schnitt

0   2   4

1. What historical reference in particular inspires you when designing a residence?
   Quelles références historiques vous inspirent en particulier lorsque vous dessinez une maison ?
   Welche historische Referenz dient Ihnen als Inspiration beim Entwurf eines Hauses?

2. What is the main factor taken into consideration when designing a residence?
   Quel facteur principal prenez-vous en considération lors de la conception d'une maison ?
   Welche Rahmenbedingungen, bzw. Faktoren sind für Sie ausschlaggebend beim Konzipieren?

3. What room inside the home do you find most interesting to design?
   Quelle pièce trouvez-vous la plus intéressante à dessiner ?
   Welchen Raum des Hauses finden Sie am spannendsten zu entwerfen?

4. What is your criteria for choosing materials and finishings in a particular room?
   Sur quels critères choisissez-vous les matériaux et les finitions d'une pièce ?
   Welche Kriterien wenden Sie bei der Entscheidung über Materialien und Oberflächen in diesem Raum an?

1. The way in which nature has been incorporated in architecture in the past is the historical reference that inspires us the most such as use of natural light and wind.

2. The majority of our work has been residences in urban areas. Thus, the main factor that is taken into consideration when designing a residence is how we can incorporate a life style of a resident to town space.

3. Our interest expands beyond designing a particular room. We are rather interested in continuity of rooms and spaces of a house.

4. We do not choose materials not only by their looks and colors but also by their touch, feel, acoustic quality, and the way they combine with other materials.

1. La référence historique qui nous inspire le plus est la manière dont, par le passé, la nature s'est intégrée dans l'architecture, avec, par exemple, l'intégration du vent et de la lumière naturelle.

2. La plupart de nos œuvres sont des résidences urbaines. Aussi, notre principale préoccupation quand nous dessinons un espace consiste à tenter d'intégrer le style de vie des occupants dans l'espace urbain.

3. Notre préoccupation s'étend au-delà de la conception d'une pièce en particulier. Nous sommes plus intéressés à la continuité entre les pièces et les espaces de la maison.

4. Nous ne choisissons pas uniquement les matériaux en raison de leur aspect et de leur couleur mais aussi à cause de leur texture, de leur qualité acoustique et de leur combinaison avec les autres matériaux.

1. Die historische Referenz, die uns am meisten inspiriert, ist die Art und Weise, wie man die Natur in die Architektur der Vergangenheit integriert hat, zum Beispiel, wie mit dem Wind oder dem Tageslicht umgegangen wurde.

2. Die meisten unserer Arbeiten sind städtische Wohnhäuser. Deshalb ist es für uns bei der Gestaltung eines Raumes sehr wichtig, den Lebensstil seiner Bewohner in die städtische Umgebung zu integrieren.

3. Unsere Interessen gehen weit über die Gestaltung eines speziellen Raumes hinaus. Uns interessiert die Kontinuität zwischen den Zimmern und Räumen einer Wohnung.

4. Wir wählen die Materialien nicht allein aufgrund ihres Aussehens und ihrer Farbe aus, sondern auch danach, wie sie sich anfühlen, nach ihren akustischen Eigenschaften und wie sie sich mit anderen Materialien kombinieren lassen.

Yasushi Ikeda was born in 1961 in Fukuoka. He studied in the Architecture School at the University of Tokyo and worked in the architectural office of Maki and Associates (1987-1995). Later, he established Ikeda Design Studio. Since 1996 he is an assistant professor in the School of Environmental Information in Keio University.
Akiko Kokubun was born in 1965 in Tokyo. She studied in the Architecture School at the University of Tokyo and worked in the architectural office of Maki and Associates (1988-1997). In 1997 she joined the Ikeda Kokubun Design Studio.

Yasushi Ikeda est né en 1961 à Fukuoka. Il a étudié à l'école d'architecture de l'université de Tokyo et travaillé à l'agence Maki and Associates (1987-1995). Il créa ensuite Ikeda Design Studio. Il est professeur assistant à l'école de l'information environnementale de l'université de Keio depuis 1996.
Akiko Kokubun est née en 1965 à Tokyo. Elle a étudié à l'école d'architecture de l'université de Tokyo et travaillé à l'agence Maki and Associates (1988-1997). En 1997, elle a rejoint l'agence Ikeda Design Studio.

Yasushi Ikeda kam 1961 in Fukuoka zur Welt. Er studierte Architektur an der Universität von Tokio und arbeitete in dem Unternehmen Maki and Associates (1987-1995). Später gründete er Ikeda Design Studio. Seit 1996 ist er assistierender Professor an der Fakultät für Umweltinformation der Keio Universität.
Akiko Kokubun kam 1965 in Tokio zur Welt. Sie studierte Architektur an der Universität von Tokio und arbeitete in dem Unternehmen Maki and Associates (1988-1997). 1997 wurde sie Mitbegründerin des Kokubun Design Studios.

The history of this project began with the need to cover the top floor of this building in order to protect the lower levels from the elements. The resulting space was later occupied by separate, individual structures. In their approach to the renovation project the architects used this concept as a point of departure to create a residence based on minimal units that were developed according to a mutual relationship. The placement of the units was based on geometric shapes that break up the building's existing straight lines. This manipulation of form helps direct the eye towards distant views, beyond the surrounding neighbors. The interior units can be expanded and adapted according to specific needs using textile panels that slide on rails. These elements can also be folded so that the spaces can almost entirely be integrated. The roof extends beyond the sides of the building to create overhanging glass projections, which show the interior work while covering projections from the lower floors of the building.

Rooftop

Holodeck.at

Vienna, Austria, 2002
Photos © Veronika Hofinger

Au début de ce projet, il y avait la nécessité de couvrir le dernier étage de l'édifice afin de protéger les étages inférieurs des intempéries, l'espace résultant ayant ensuite été aménagé. Dans leur approche de la rénovation, les architectes ont utilisé ce concept comme point de départ pour créer une résidence qui s'appuie sur des unités minimales se développant suivant une relation mutuelle. La disposition des unités se fonde

Die Grundlage dieser Planung war die Notwendigkeit, das Dach eines letzten Stockwerkes zu decken, um die unteren Stockwerke vor Wettereinflüssen zu schützen. Der dadurch entstandene Raum wurde allmählich von einzelnen, individuellen Elementen eingenommen. Die Architekten betrachteten dieses Renovierungsprojekt als Ausgangspunkt für die Erschaffung eines Wohnraumes, der auf minimalen Einheiten basiert, die sich gemeinsam

sur des formes géométriques qui brisent les lignes existantes du bâtiment. Cette manipulation des formes aide à orienter le regard vers un panorama lointain, au-delà du proche voisinage. Les unités intérieures peuvent s'étendre et s'adapter en fonction de besoins spécifiques à l'aide de panneaux de toile glissant sur des rails. Ils peuvent également se replier de manière à intégrer entièrement les espaces. La toiture s'étend au-delà des limites du bâtiment en surplombs vitrés qui révèlent l'intérieur tout en couvrant les projections des étages inférieurs.

entwickeln. Die Anordnung der Teile geht von einer Geometrie aus, die die rechtwinkligen Linien des existierenden Gebäudes bricht. Mit dieser formalen Geste wird der Blick auf das weit entfernte Panorama gelenkt, über den umgebenden Gebäuden gelegen. Die inneren Einheiten können mithilfe von Stoffpaneelen, die auf Führungen verschoben werden, für die jeweilige Nutzung erweitert oder verändert werden. Diese Elemente können auch gefaltet werden, so dass die Einheiten praktisch zu einem einzigen Raum werden können. Das Dach erstreckt sich außerhalb der Wohnung in Form von gläsernen Vorsprüngen, und zeigt somit die äußeren und inneren Eingriffe und deckt gleichzeitig die Wohnung und die unteren Stockwerke des Gebäudes.

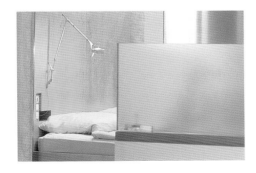

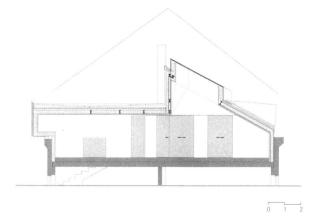

Ground floor

Rez-de-chaussée

Erdgeschoss

Section

Coupe

Schnitt

0   1   2

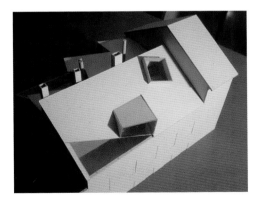

Model
Maquette
Modell

1. What historical reference in particular inspires you when designing a residence?
   Quelles références historiques vous inspirent en particulier lorsque vous dessinez une maison ?
   Welche historische Referenz dient Ihnen als Inspiration beim Entwurf eines Hauses?

2. What is the main factor taken into consideration when designing a residence?
   Quel facteur principal prenez-vous en considération lors de la conception d'une maison ?
   Welche Rahmenbedingungen, bzw. Faktoren sind für Sie ausschlaggebend beim Konzipieren?

3. What room inside the home do you find most interesting to design?
   Quelle pièce trouvez-vous la plus intéressante à dessiner ?
   Welchen Raum des Hauses finden Sie am spannendsten zu entwerfen?

4. What is your criteria for choosing materials and finishings in a particular room?
   Sur quels critères choisissez-vous les matériaux et les finitions d'une pièce ?
   Welche Kriterien wenden Sie bei der Entscheidung über Materialien und Oberflächen in diesem Raum an?

1. The continuity and complexity of spaces and the social interactivity in the historical 'medina' as well as the principle of the courtyard house.

2. The adaption of the program 'housing' to the complexity of the clients desires combined with the particularities of the site.

3. The continuum of spaces and their flexible arrangement following the functional and emotional demands of the client.

4. To emphasize the conceptual idea.

1. La continuité et la complexité des espaces et l'interactivité sociale dans la médina historique ainsi que le principe de maison avec patio.

2. L'adaptation du programme à la complexité des désirs des clients ainsi qu'aux particularités du site.

3. La continuité des espaces et leur arrangement flexible suivant les demandes fonctionnelles et émotionnelles du client.

4. Accentuer l'idée conceptuelle.

1. Die Kontinuität und die Vielschichtigkeit der Räume und die soziale Dialogfähigkeit in den historischen, arabischen Altstädten als das Konzept eines Hauses mit Garten.

2. Die Anpassung der Wohnprogramme an die Vielschichtigkeit der Wünsche der Kunden in Kombination mit den Eigenschaften des Grundstückes.

3. Die Kontinuität der Räume und die flexible Verteilung, die den funktionellen und emotionalen Wünschen des Kunden entspricht.

4. Die abstrakte Idee unterstreichen.

Holodeck.at is a design office founded in 1998 by Marlies Breuss, Michael Ogertsching and Susanne Schmall. She left the firm at the beginning of 2001, gaining additional experience at studios in Los Angeles, Barcelona, and Tokyo. Her philosophy is based on a conceptual and logical plan that focuses on restructuring projects and developing specific functions. Holodeck.at creates the design tools required for their projects by collecting and researching information on the particular location.

Holodeck.at est une agence de décoration fondée en 1998 par Marlies Breuss, Michael Ogertsching et Susanne Schmall. Cette dernière a quitté l'agence début 2001. Avec des expériences à Los Angeles, Barcelone et Tokyo, la philosophie de l'agence se fonde, d'un point de vue conceptuel et logique, sur la restructuration des projets et le développement de fonctions spécifiques. Holodeck.at crée les outils de design nécessaires à ses projets en rassemblant et en recherchant des informations sur le site.

Holodeck.at ist ein Architekturbüro, das von Marlies Breuss, Michael Ogertsching und Susanne Schmall 1998 gegründet wurde. Susanne Schmall verließ die Firma 2001. Die Architekten haben durch Studien in Los Angeles, Barcelona und Tokio Erfahrung gesammelt. Die Unternehmensphilosophie beruht auf einem konzeptuellen und programmatischen Schema, hauptsächlich widmet man sich der Neustrukturierung von Wohnräumen und der Entwicklung spezifischer Funktionen. Durch das Speichern und Filtern von Informationen über den Standort werden die Gestaltungswerkzeuge für die einzelnen Aufträge geschaffen.

The location of the Ray 1 project, on the top floor of a 1960's office building in the center of Vienna's fourth district, served as a reference and an inspiration for the design of the project. The architect's design, which inevitably had to take into account the strict regulations regarding the coverings of buildings, did not fit into the typical mold, but was approached as a reinterpretation of these kinds of regulations. In order to apply the design concept, a steel skeleton was used to evenly distribute the load on the building's original structure. The gable carries the main weight while the other metal parts act as frames for the glass covering. The result is surprisingly light and creates a structure that is particularly interesting in relation to the surrounding urban setting. The form of the structure itself, as well as the permanent relationship with the surrounding landscape, creates a dynamic atmosphere in the interior and an opportunity to experience the outside from terraces or through large openings.

Ray 1

Delugan_Meissl

Vienna, Austria, 2003
Photos © Rupert Steiner

L'emplacement de Ray 1, au sommet d'un immeuble de bureaux des années 1960, et au cœur du quatrième arrondissement de Vienne, a servi de référence et de stimulus lors de la conception du projet. Le design des architectes, qui devaient inévitablement tenir compte de la stricte réglementation concernant la toiture des bâtiments, ne rentrait pas dans le cadre habituel mais s'affirmait comme une réinterprétation de ces règles.

Der Standort des Projektes Ray 1 im obersten Stockwerk eines Bürogebäudes aus den Sechzigerjahren, inmitten des vierten Bezirks von Wien, diente als Referenzpunkt und Inspiration für Durchführung des Projektes. Bei der Gestaltung konnten die strengen Verordnungen für die Gestaltung der Dächer nicht umgangen werden. Diese werden jedoch nicht als Einschränkungen aufgefasst, sondern sie werden einfach auf kreative Weise neu inter-

Pour pouvoir réaliser ce projet, il fallut d'abord poser une charpente en acier sur la structure originelle du bâtiment afin de répartir également la charge. Le gâble reçoit le poids principal tandis que les autres parties métalliques servent de charpente à la couverture vitrée. Le résultat est étonnamment léger et montre une structure particulièrement intéressante par rapport à l'environnement urbain. La forme de la charpente elle-même, ainsi que la relation permanente avec le paysage environnant, créent une atmosphère dynamique à l'intérieur et permet de découvrir l'extérieur depuis des terrasses ou de larges baies.

pretiert. Um das Designkonzept auf die Originalstruktur des Gebäudes übertragen zu können, wurde ein Stahlskelett gewählt, über das die Lasten gleichmäßig auf die Mauern des Gebäudes übertragen werden. Die Hauptlasten werden von der Seitenwand getragen, während die übrigen Elemente aus Metall als Rahmen für die Hülle aus Glas dienen. Das Ergebnis wirkt überraschend leicht und es entstand ein Objekt, das in seiner unmittelbaren Umgebung sehr interessant wirkt. Die Form der Struktur selbst und die ständige Beziehung zu der umgebenden Landschaft schaffen eine dynamische Atmosphäre im Inneren und geben die Möglichkeit, außen mithilfe von Terrassen und großen Öffnungen zu experimentieren.

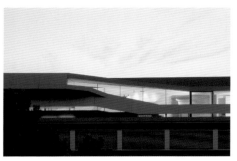

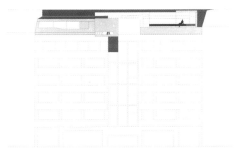
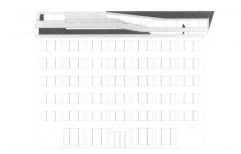

Elevations
Élévations
Aufrisse

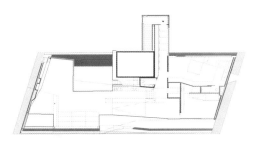
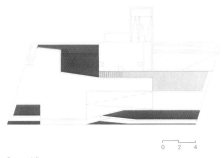

```
0   2   4
```

First floor
Premier étage
Erster Stock

Second floor
Deuxième étage
Zweiter Stock

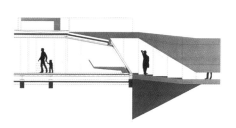
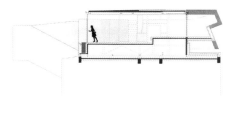

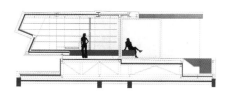
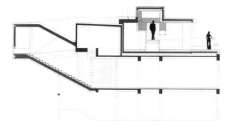

Sections
Coupes
Schnitte

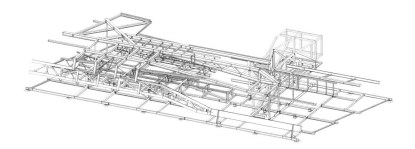

Axonometry

Axonométrie

Axonometrie

Transversal section

Coupe transversale

Querschnitt

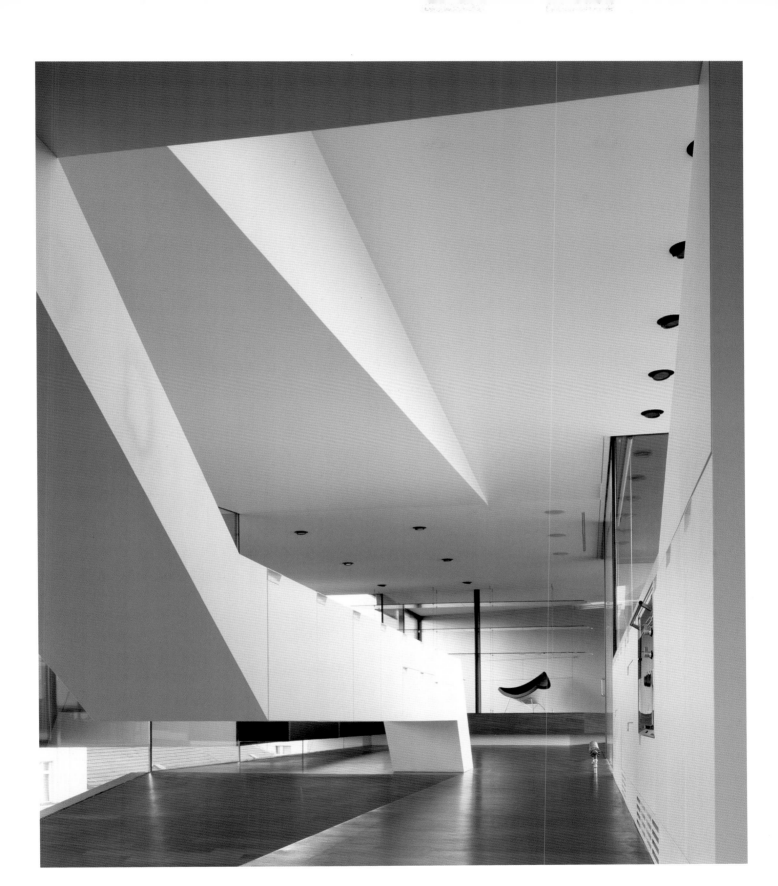

1. What historical reference in particular inspires you when designing a residence?
   Quelles références historiques vous inspirent en particulier lorsque vous dessinez une maison ?
   Welche historische Referenz dient Ihnen als Inspiration beim Entwurf eines Hauses?

2. What is the main factor taken into consideration when designing a residence?
   Quel facteur principal prenez-vous en considération lors de la conception d'une maison ?
   Welche Rahmenbedingungen, bzw. Faktoren sind für Sie ausschlaggebend beim Konzipieren?

3. What room inside the home do you find most interesting to design?
   Quelle pièce trouvez-vous la plus intéressante à dessiner ?
   Welchen Raum des Hauses finden Sie am spannendsten zu entwerfen?

4. What is your criteria for choosing materials and finishings in a particular room?
   Sur quels critères choisissez-vous les matériaux et les finitions d'une pièce ?
   Welche Kriterien wenden Sie bei der Entscheidung über Materialien und Oberflächen in diesem Raum an?

---

1. The architecture of Oscar Niemeyer and John Lautner.

2. In our concepts a building is always conceived as one aspect of something greater as existing within a spatial context. The design has its starting point in the genius loci.

3. A combination of living room and kitchen – we find it highly interesting how rooms interact with each other and how we could achieve the interior space as a flowing internal continuum whose various functional areas are defined by different floor levels, zones, or niches without using spatial or visual separators.

4. The materials we choose reflect and support the specific demanded use of each particular room and their haptic dimension is very important to us. In most cases we use materials in their original color in order to give a starting point for an individual colorful occupation.

---

1. L'architecture d'Oscar Niemeyer et de John Lautner.

2. Dans notre conception, un bâtiment est toujours envisagé autant comme un élément inscrit dans quelque chose de plus grand que comme appartenant à un contexte spatial. La conception prend son point de départ dans l'esprit du lieu.

3. La combinaison salle à manger et cuisine. Nous trouvons très intéressant la manière dont les pièces interfèrent entre elles et comment nous pouvons créer un flux continu dans l'espace intérieur, dont les différentes zones fonctionnelles sont définies par les différents niveaux du sol, les différentes zones ou niches sans recourir à des séparations spatiales ou visuelles.

4. les matériaux que nous choisissons reflètent et accentuent l'usage spécifique de chaque pièce, et leur dimension tactile est très importante pour nous. Dans la majorité des cas, nous utilisons les matériaux dans leur couleur originelle afin de créer un point de départ pour une appropriation individuelle.

---

1. Die Architektur von Oscar Niemeyer und John Lautner.

2. Es ist unsere Auffassung, dass ein Gebäude immer als ein Element innerhalb einer existierenden, größeren Einheit in einem räumlichen Kontextes entworfen wird. Der Ausgangspunkt für die Gestaltung ist der Geist, der an dem Ort herrscht.

3. Eine Kombination von Wohnzimmer und Küche finden wir sehr interessant, da hier die verschiedenen Räume miteinander in Beziehung stehen. So wird ein durchgehender, fließender innerer Raum geschaffen, dessen verschiedenen Bereiche durch die Fußböden und Zonen oder Öffnungen auf verschiedener Höhe definiert sind, ohne dass dazu räumliche oder visuelle teilende Elemente notwendig sind.

4. Die von uns ausgewählten Materialien spiegeln die spezifische Nutzung jedes Zimmer wieder und verstärken sie. Die taktile Dimension ist uns sehr wichtig. In den meisten Fällen verwenden wir Materialien, ohne ihre Farbe zu verändern, um so einen Ausgangspunkt für eine individuelle Besetzung zu schaffen.

Elke Delugan-Meissl (Linz, Austria) and Roman Delugan (Merano, Italy) joined to found their own architectural office in 1993. If there is a principle that guides their design method it would probably be the landscape. For them, a building is always seen as another aspect of something much larger that forms part of a spatial context, and not just a single structure. The design of each element is approached as a synthesis of the setting, while attempting to contribute something that would complement it. Their work encompasses a wide range of residential projects.

Elke Delugan-Meissl (Linz, Autriche) et Roman Delugan (Merano, Italie) se sont associés pour créer leur propre agence d'architecture en 1993. Le principe essentiel qui guide leur méthode de conception est probablement le paysage. Pour eux, un bâtiment est toujours considéré non comme une simple structure mais comme un autre aspect de quelque chose de beaucoup plus grand appartenant au contexte spatial. La conception de chaque élément est envisagée comme une synthèse de l'environnement et une création qui vient le compléter. Leur œuvre comprend un large éventail de projets résidentiels.

Elke Delugan-Meissl (Linz, Österreich) und Roman Delugan (Meran, Italien) gründeten 1993 gemeinsam ein Architekturstudio. Falls es ein Prinzip gäbe, nach dem sich ihre Designmethode richtet, so wäre dies wahrscheinlich die Landschaft. Für diese Architekten ist ein Gebäude immer ein Aspekt einer größeren Einheit. Es gehört in einen räumlichen Kontext und ist keine einsame Struktur. Die Gestaltung jedes Elementes wird als die Synthese der Umgebung aufgefasst; gleichzeitig soll die Umgebung ergänzt werden. Sie haben bereits zahlreiche Projekte für Wohnanlagen verwirklicht.

This project consisted of enlarging seven units in an existing residential complex. Five of the units are arrayed in a long building while the other two are independent structures around an open patio. The model of the residences is based on the original plan, consisting of three levels inside each residence. The interrelated and open floor plan allows for a variety of uses. The connection between the spaces is emphasized by the double-height ceiling, while their close relationship to the exterior is enhanced by the large windows that open to each unit's small private garden. The old industrial lofts not only inspired the floor plan and the use of the space, they also served as a reference when the time came to select the materials and finishes. Wood, metal, brick, and glass are predominant, and the materials are always left exposed to impart an industrial character to the interior of each living space.

Bay Cities Lofts: Phase II

Mark Mack Architects

Venice, CA, USA, 2003
Photos © Undine Pröhl

Ce projet consiste en l'agrandissement de sept appartements dans un complexe résidentiel existant. Cinq unités sont regroupées dans un édifice longitudinal, tandis que les deux autres se projettent comme volumes indépendants autour d'un patio ouvert. La typologie des pièces est fondée sur le plan original et propose une solution verticale sur trois niveaux à l'intérieur de chaque résidence. Chaque unité profite diversement

Dieses Projekt besteht in der Erweiterung von sieben Wohnungen in einem bereits existierenden Gebäude. Fünf dieser Wohnungen liegen in einem längs verlaufenden Gebäude, die anderen beiden sind unabhängige Bauten um einen offenen Hof. Die Wohnungen wurden im gleichen Stil wie das Originalgebäude gestaltet. Es wurde eine vertikale Lösung vorgeschlagen, bei der in jedem Wohnhaus drei Ebenen vorgesehen sind. Die offenen, mit-

des espaces créés, ouverts et interconnectés. Le lien entre ces espaces est mis en valeur par un plafond double hauteur tandis que la relation étroite avec l'extérieur est assurée par une large baie ouvrant sur les petits jardins privatifs de chaque appartement. L'exemple des anciens lofts industriels a servi non seulement à configurer la distribution et l'usage de l'espace, mais a servi aussi de référent dans le choix des matériaux et des finitions. Toujours apparents, bois, métal, brique, et verre prédominent et donnent son caractère industriel à chaque espace de vie.

einander verbundenen Räume können auf verschiedene Weise benutzt werden. Die Verbindung zwischen den Räumen und die enge Verbindung mit dem Äußeren wird noch durch die doppelte Höhe und die großen Fenster unterstrichen, die zu den kleinen Privatgärten jedes Wohnhauses zeigen. Sowohl die Verteilung und die Nutzung der Räume als auch die Auswahl der Materialien und Gestaltungselemente ist vom Stil alter Fabriketagen inspiriert. Hauptsächlich werden Holz, Ziegelstein, Metall und Glas verwendet. Diese Materialien sind immer sichtbar, was den industriellen Charakter im Innenausbau der Häuser unterstreicht.

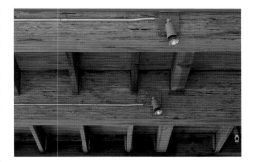

Ground floor

Rez-de-chaussée

Erdgeschoss

First floor

Premier étage

Erster Stock

Second floor

Deuxième étage

Zweiter Stock

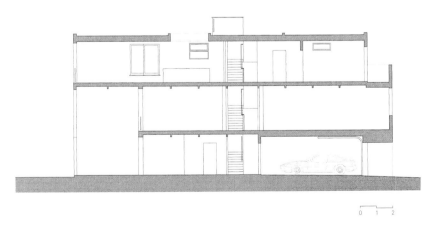

0 1 2

Transversal section
Coupe transversale
Querschnitt

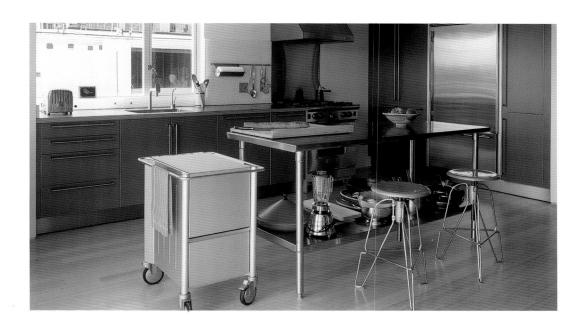

Mark Mack, along with his former partner Andrew Batey, earned his reputation as an architect in California mainly for his single-family home and villa designs in the early 1980's. He established his own office in San Francisco in 1984 and then moved to Venice, California in 1993. His approach to design is influenced by his academic work and restless curiosity. He was a professor in the School of Architecture at the University of California, Los Angeles. He was also a cofounder of Archetype Magazine and has contributed numerous articles to different magazines.

Mark Mack, avec son ancien associé Andrew Batey, a forgé sa réputation d'architecte en Californie principalement grâce à ses maisons et à ses villas au début des années 1980. Il a créé sa propre agence à San Francisco en 1984 puis est parti s'installer à Venice en 1993. Son approche du design est influencée par son œuvre académique et sa curiosité insatiable. Il a été professeur à l'école d'architecture de l'université de Californie à Los Angeles. Également cofondateur d'*Archetype Magazine*, il a publié de nombreux articles dans plusieurs publications.

Mark Mack begann seine Karriere Anfang der Achtzigerjahre mit der Planung von Einfamilienhäusern und Villen in Kalifornien zusammen mit seinem ehemaligen Teilhaber Andrew Batey. 1984 gründete er in San Francisco sein eigenes Unternehmen, das er 1993 nach Venice, Kalifornien, verlegte. Seine Interessen und seine akademische Arbeit beeinflussen stark seinen Gestaltungsstil. Er war Professor am Fachbereich Architektur der Universität von Kalifornien in Los Angeles. Ebenso ist er Mitbegründer der Zeitschrift Archetype Magazine, in der er zahlreiche Artikel veröffentlicht hat.

APARTMENTS

APPARTEMENTS / WOHNUNGEN

This luxury apartment in the corner of the 49th floor of a building located on New York's Fifth Avenue has impressive views of Rockefeller Center and Midtown Manhattan. The clients, a German industrial magnate and his wife, envisioned an apartment characterized by light and spatial harmony that would be an urban refuge during their frequent visits to the city. The design of the interior renovation proposed minimal construction with a fluid integration between the different computerized systems to create an ideal setting for modern living. The design concept consisted of a light, crystal-clear space that functioned as an observatory of the metropolitan collage. The audiovisual system is contained in a structure that acts as the pivot point for the distribution of the main living and dining areas and the master bedroom. The atmosphere of the interior is created with several luxury materials and a basic palette dominated by white plaster, marble from Yugoslavia, and translucent crystal. A glass wall formed by two white enameled panels illuminated from below separates the kitchen from the dining area. The design balances the use of light, the forms, and the materials and allows them to co-exist in harmony in this Minimalist environment.

Olympic Tower Residence

Gabellini Associates

New York, NY, USA, 2003
Photos © Paul Warchol

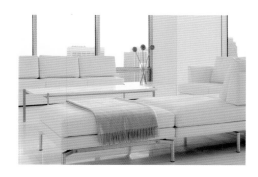

Ce luxueux appartement, qui occupe le coin du 49ᵉ étage d'un building situé sur la 5ᵉ Avenue à New York, jouit d'un impressionnant panorama sur le Rockefeller Center et Midtown Manhattan. Les clients, un magnat de l'industrie allemand et son épouse, imaginaient un appartement clair et spatialement harmonieux pour leur servir de refuge lors de leurs fréquents passages en ville. La rénovation intérieure proposée leur présen-

Von diesem luxuriösen Appartement auf der Ecke eines 49. Stockwerks in einem Gebäude an der 5th Avenue von New York aus hat man einen überwältigenden Blick auf das Rockefeller Center und Midtown Manhattan. Die Kunden sind ein deutscher Industriemagnat und seine Ehefrau. Sie wünschten sich eine Wohnung, die von Klarheit und räumlicher Harmonie geprägt ist, und ihnen als Zufluchtsort bei ihren häufigen Besuchen in dieser

tait un projet minimaliste avec une intégration fluide des différents systèmes offrant un cadre idéal pour un mode de vie moderne. Le concept était de créer un volume cristallin et léger qui servirait d'observatoire du collage métropolitain. Le volume où sont regroupés les systèmes audiovisuels est l'espace central d'où sont distribuées la pièce de séjour, la salle à manger et la chambre principale. Le luxe des matériaux et la palette de couleurs basiques due au plâtre blanc, au marbre de Yougoslavie et au verre translucide créent l'atmosphère intérieure. Une paroi de verre, habillée de deux panneaux laqués blanc éclairés par en dessous, sépare la cuisine de la salle à manger. En les équilibrant, la décoration fait coexister harmonieusement lumière, formes et matériaux dans cet environnement minimaliste.

Stadt dienen sollte. Die Gestaltung der Räume ist sehr minimalistisch und es findet eine fließende Integration zwischen verschiedenen, intelligenten Systemen statt, um eine ideale Umgebung für das moderne Leben zu schaffen. Die Gestalter schlugen kristallartige, leicht wirkende Räume vor, die zu einer Art Observatorium der Großstadt-Collage werden. In einem Raum befinden sich die audiovisuellen Systeme, von hier aus werden die Bereiche für das Wohnen, Essen und Schlafen organisiert. Die Atmosphäre ist von luxuriösen Materialien geprägt, die Farbpalette reicht vom Weiß des Gipses über die Töne des jugoslawischen Marmors bis zum durchsichtigen Glas. Eine Glaswand, die von zwei weiß emaillierten und von unten beleuchteten Platten gebildet wird, trennt die Küche vom Speisezimmer. Die Gestaltung spielt mit dem Licht, den Formen und den Materialien, damit sie sich harmonisch in diese minimalistische Umgebung einpassen.

Plan
Plan
Grundriss

After finishing his studies at the Rhode Island School of Design in 1980 and complementing them at the Architectural Association of London, Michael Gabellini founded Gabellini Associates en 1991. Gabellini is known for his luxurious, elegant designs in which space and light are the main components. He has designed several boutiques for the most prestigious companies of the fashion world. His studies in art led him to carry out several projects for galleries and museums. In residential design he uses an esthetic that mixes the sophisticated and the casual to create a comfortable environment.

Michael Gabellini a fondé Gabellini Associates en 1991 après avoir achevé ses études en 1980 à la Rhode Island School of Design, complétées par un passage à l'Architectural Association de Londres. Gabellini s'est fait connaître par ses décorations luxueuses et élégantes, où l'espace et la lumière tiennent le premier rôle. Il a ainsi conçu de nombreuses boutiques pour les plus grands noms de la mode. Ses études l'ont également conduit à mener à bien plusieurs projets pour des galeries et des musées. Pour des appartements, son esthétique associe sophistication et désinvolture pour créer un environnement confortable.

Nachdem Michael Gabellini 1980 sein Architekturstudium an der Rhode Island School of Design abgeschlossen hatte, und sich an der Architectural Association in London weitergebildet hatte, gründete er 1991 Gabellini Associates. Gabellini ist für luxuriöse, elegante und elementare Entwürfe bekannt, in denen Licht und Raum die wichtigsten Elemente sind. Aufgrund seines Interesses für die moderne Kunst hat er auch verschiedene Projekte für Museen und Galerien durchgeführt. Die von ihm gestalteten Wohnungen zeichnen sich dadurch aus, dass sie Edles mit spontaneren Elementen verbinden.

The architects describe this project as two halves that had functioned independently, which were combined to form a large and light-filled single unit. There were no restrictions other than the need for two bedrooms, so the architects designed a showcase that spanned the length of the house. The building was stripped to its foundation, and a long axis was created in the upper floor to articulate the different spaces in the residence. A double high gallery connected the two levels, which before were completely isolated from each other. An elegant metal stairway that looks like a piece of sculpture was added to the gallery, separating the salon from the library. The few colors and materials, separated from each other, enhance this sense of space. The floor of the more public lower level is made of sandstone, while the floor of the upper level, where the private rooms are located, is covered with wood parquet. The beige tone of the walls, halfway between the color of the stone and that of the wood, creates a monolithic effect of great tranquility.

House T

Frei Architekten

Kloten, Switzerland, 2000
Photos © Bruno Helbling / zapaimages

Les architectes décrivent leur projet comme deux moitiés ayant fonctionné de manière indépendante et qu'ils assemblèrent pour ne former qu'un seul vaste et lumineux appartement. N'ayant aucune autre consigne que de créer deux chambres, ils conçurent une promenade architectonique à travers les pièces en débarrassant le bâtiment de ses fondations et en créant à l'étage un axe longitudinal qui articule les différents espaces de l'ap-

Die Architekten beschreiben dieses Gebäude als zwei Hälften, die unabhängig voneinander funktionierten, und aus denen man eine einzige, weite und helle Wohnung gemacht hat. Außer der Tatsache, dass es zwei Schlafzimmer geben musste, gab es keine andere Vorgabe für die Architekten, die diesen Eingriff in Form eines architektonischen Spaziergangs durch die Räume des Hauses angingen. Dazu wurde das Haus ganz geleert und eine

partement, tandis qu'une galerie en pleine hauteur relie entre eux les deux niveaux de la maison, auparavant complètement indépendants. Dans cette galerie, un élégant escalier de métal, comme une sculpture, sépare le salon de la bibliothèque. Couleurs et matières distinctes augmentent cette impression d'espace. Le sol du niveau inférieur, à usage plutôt public, est réalisé en grès, tandis que celui de l'étage, où sont aménagées les pièces privatives, est couvert de parquet. La tonalité beige des murs, entre la couleur de la pierre et celle du bois, crée un effet monolithique d'une grande sérénité.

Längsachse im oberen Teil eingeführt, an der entlang sich die verschiedenen Räume gliedern. Eine Galerie in doppelter Höhe verbindet die beiden Stockwerke, die vorher absolut unabhängig voneinander waren, miteinander. Auf dieser Galerie befindet sich eine feine Metalltreppe, die wie eine Skulptur wahrgenommen wird und gleichzeitig das Wohnzimmer von der Bibliothek trennt. Diese Raumidee wird von wenig Farben, die voneinander getrennt sind, begleitet. Der Boden des Erdgeschosses, das auch von Besuchern benutzt wird, ist aus Sandstein, während der Boden des Obergeschosses, in dem sich die Privaträume befinden, mit Holzparkett belegt ist. Die Wände sind beige, die Farbe vermittelt zwischen der des Steines und der des Holzes. So entsteht eine sehr einheitlich wirkende und somit beruhigende Wirkung.

1. What historical reference in particular inspires you when designing a residence?
Quelles références historiques vous inspirent en particulier lorsque vous dessinez une maison ?
Welche historische Referenz dient Ihnen als Inspiration beim Entwurf eines Hauses?

2. What is the main factor taken into consideration when designing a residence?
Quel facteur principal prenez-vous en considération lors de la conception d'une maison ?
Welche Rahmenbedingungen, bzw. Faktoren sind für Sie ausschlaggebend beim Konzipieren?

3. What room inside the home do you find most interesting to design?
Quelle pièce trouvez-vous la plus intéressante à dessiner ?
Welchen Raum des Hauses finden Sie am spannendsten zu entwerfen?

4. What is your criteria for choosing materials and finishings in a particular room?
Sur quels critères choisissez-vous les matériaux et les finitions d'une pièce ?
Welche Kriterien wenden Sie bei der Entscheidung über Materialien und Oberflächen in diesem Raum an?

1. Perhaps it is the buildings that were constructed over generations without a particular plan. Houses that have been subject to changes, adaptations, and additions in response to the needs of their occupants. I find the pursuit of modernization, where form rigorously follows function, to be an overly confining, almost boring approach.

2. The location. The building can make the place and the place can make the building; I am interested in this type of dialogue.

3. Every connecting space in a house. The rooms that can survive without having a specific function designated by the contractor.

4. The most interesting secondary rooms are those that do not have to conform to any particular function or material. The unique characteristics of each room, together with a certain atmosphere, develop during the creative process.

1. Peut-être tous ces bâtiments qui ont été construits pendant des générations sans plan particulier. Des maisons qui ont subi des changements, des adaptations et des additions pour répondre aux besoins de leurs occupants. La recherche de la modernité, où la forme suit rigoureusement la fonction, me paraît être une approche particulièrement limitée et presque ennuyeuse.

2. Le lieu. Ce qui m'intéresse c'est la dialectique selon laquelle un bâtiment peut faire le lieu et un lieu le bâtiment.

3. Tous les espaces de liaison d'une maison. Les pièces qui peuvent exister sans avoir de fonction spécifique attribuée par le maître d'œuvre.

4. Les pièces secondaires les plus intéressantes sont celles qui n'ont pas besoin de se conformer à une fonction ou à un matériau particulier. Le caractère unique de chaque pièce, ainsi que son atmosphère, se détermine au cours du processus de création.

1. Vielleicht sind es diejenigen Bauwerke, welche ohne ersichtlichen Gesamtplan über mehrere Generationen entstanden sind. Häuser, welche sowohl bezüglich Nutzer wie auch bezüglich Nutzung Änderungen, Anpassungen und Erweiterungen erfahren haben. Die Forderung der Moderne, wo Form strikt der Funktion zu folgen hat, scheint mir zu einengend, gar langweilig. Alles bleibt ablesbar und voraussehbar.

2. Der Ort. Mich interessiert diese Dialektik, dass ein Gebäude den Ort machen kann sowie eben auch der Ort das Gebäude macht.

3. Alle Zwischenräume eines Hauses. Es sind dies diejenigen Räume des Hauses, welche es gegenüber dem Raumprogramm des Bauherrn schaffen, ohne bestimmte Nutzungszuordnung zu überleben.

4. Die spannendsten Raumfolgen sind diejenigen, bei welchen nicht ein einheitliches Materialkonzept durchgezogen werden muss. Im Verlauf des Entwurfsprozesses schälen sich für die jeweiligen Räume spezifische Eigenschaften und schließlich eine Atmosphäre heraus.

Leo Frei, founder of Frei Architekten, was born in Zurich in 1958, where he also pursued his architecture studies. After earning his degree in 1983 he added a Master of Architecture degree from the Technological Institute in Atlanta. After working in different architectural firms for several years, he started his own office in 1991, in Zurich and Stäfa. He complements his work as an architect with academic duties as a professor, assistant, and instructor in various Swiss universities.

Leo Frei, fondateur de Frei Architekten, est né à Zurich en 1958, où il a poursuivi ses études d'architecture. Ayant obtenu son diplôme en 1983, il réussit le Master d'Architecture du Technologicial Institute d'Atlanta. Après avoir travaillé plusieurs années pour différents architectes, il créa en 1991 sa propre agence à Zurich et Stäfa. En plus de son travail d'architecte, il est également professeur, assistant et formateur dans différentes universités suisses.

Leo Frei, der Gründer von Frei Architekten, kam 1958 in Zürich auf die Welt, wo er auch Architektur studierte. Nach Abschluss seines Diploms im Jahr 1983 erwarb er noch einen Master am Technological Institute in Atlanta. Nachdem er mehrere Jahre lang in verschiedenen Architekturbüros mitgearbeitet hatte, gründete er 1991 sein eigenes Unternehmen in Zürich und Stäfa. Seine Arbeit als Architekt ergänzt er mit seiner Lehrtätigkeit als Professor, Assistent und Tutor an verschiedenen Universitäten in der Schweiz.

For this project the client wanted to create a private residence by combining two typical commercial mews in London. This was a complicated task due to the difficult conditions on both the exterior and interior of the original structures. The first challenge was to obtain permission from the local authorities to change the property's zoning from commercial to residential. The restrictions of the façade and the lack of any space around the property called for a strategy that consisted of opening up the rear of the building as much as possible and creating light and subtle barriers inside. This approach created a space that was open, ventilated, and well lit. Several skylights, as well as the placement of a few interior mirrors, brighten the space and make it feel even more open. The remodeling also created a cohesive composition from the previous series of subdivided spaces, which were different in character from each other. Most of the interior walls were removed and a common language was created based on the consistent use of materials and finishes throughout the two units. The rich color and texture of the materials create a soft, warm atmosphere that is more appropriate for the new residential function.

London Mews Conversion

co-labarchitects

London, UK, 2003
Photos © Mat Jessop

Pour ce projet, le client voulait créer un appartement en réunissant deux venelles commerciales typiques de Londres (d'anciennes écuries). La tâche fut compliquée en raison du mauvais état des structures originelles, intérieures comme extérieures. Le premier obstacle fut d'obtenir des autorités l'autorisation de changer la destination de l'immeuble, de commercial à résidentiel. Les contingences en façade et le manque d'espace autour

Der Kunde gab eine Privatwohnung in Auftrag, für die zwei kommerziell genutzte Mews (ehemalige umgebaute Stallungen) in London vereint und renoviert werden sollten. Das war aufgrund der schwierigen, äußeren und inneren Struktur der Originalgebäude eine komplizierte Aufgabe. Zunächst musste man überhaupt eine Baugenehmigung bekommen, um aus einem Geschäftsgebäude ein Wohnhaus machen zu dürfen. An der Fassade durfte

de la propriété conduisirent à ouvrir le plus possible l'arrière du bâtiment et à créer un cloisonnement léger et subtil à l'intérieur. Cette approche créa un espace ouvert, ventilé et bien éclairé. Plusieurs puits de lumière et des miroirs judicieusement placés augmentent ainsi la perception du volume. Ce remodelage propose également une composition plus cohérente que celle qu'offrait précédemment la suite de subdivisions, dont les espaces présentaient chacun un caractère différent. Une fois la plupart des cloisons enlevées, un langage commun fut élaboré entre les deux unités en s'appuyant sur les matériaux et les finitions. Les matières, de couleur et de texture riches, procurent une atmosphère douce et chaleureuse tout à fait appropriée à la nouvelle fonction résidentielle.

nicht viel geändert werden und außen gab es keinen Platz, deshalb musste der Raum so weit wie möglich nach hinten geöffnet werden, und die inneren Abtrennungen sollten mehrdeutig und leicht sein. So entstanden offene, luftige und helle Räume. Durch verschiedene Dachfenster und Spiegel im Inneren wird das Licht verteilt und der Eindruck von offenen Räumen noch verstärkt. Außerdem wurde Nachdruck auf eine zusammenhängende Komposition der Räume gelegt, die vorher unterteilt und sehr verschieden waren. Das erreichte man durch den Abriss der meisten Innenwände und den Einsatz von ähnlichen Materialien und Stilen in beiden Einheiten. Die Materialien mit ihrer reichen Textur und Farbigkeit schaffen eine sanfte und warme, wohnliche Atmosphäre in den neuen Räumen.

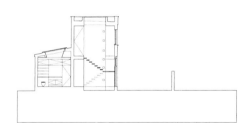

Ground floor

Rez-de-chaussée

Erdgeschoss

First floor

Premier étage

Erster Stock

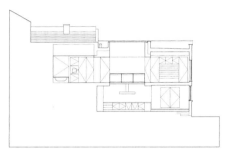

Sections

Coupes

Schnitte

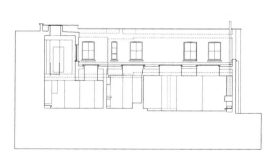

Elevations

Élévations

Aufrisse

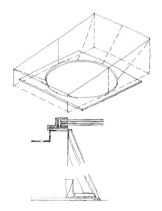
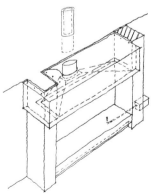
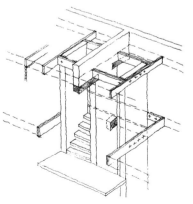

Details
Détails
Details

1. What historical reference in particular inspires you when designing a residence?
   Quelles références historiques vous inspirent en particulier lorsque vous dessinez une maison ?
   Welche historische Referenz dient Ihnen als Inspiration beim Entwurf eines Hauses?

2. What is the main factor taken into consideration when designing a residence?
   Quel facteur principal prenez-vous en considération lors de la conception d'une maison ?
   Welche Rahmenbedingungen, bzw. Faktoren sind für Sie ausschlaggebend beim Konzipieren?

3. What room inside the home do you find most interesting to design?
   Quelle pièce trouvez-vous la plus intéressante à dessiner ?
   Welchen Raum des Hauses finden Sie am spannendsten zu entwerfen?

4. What is your criteria for choosing materials and finishings in a particular room?
   Sur quels critères choisissez-vous les matériaux et les finitions d'une pièce ?
   Welche Kriterien wenden Sie bei der Entscheidung über Materialien und Oberflächen in diesem Raum an?

1. The house of John Soane in London was designed to house his large collection of art and antiquities. The plasticity and ambiguity of the spaces and the manipulation of natural daylight raises the architecture to a spiritual level.

2. The aspirations of the client is the most important aspect of designing a residence. The goal of the designer is to exceed these aspirations and realize space beyond the client's own imagination.

3. The living space is the social hub of all houses and it's relationship to the other spaces is critical. The definition of this space is all encompassing, it can sometimes be the only room in a studio apartment.

4. We are moving away from white minimalist space by using color and texture more and more in our projects.

1. La maison de John Soane à Londres fut conçue pour abriter sa vaste collection d'art et d'antiquités. La plasticité et l'ambiguïté des espaces et la manipulation de la lumière naturelle élèvent ici l'architecture à un niveau spirituel.

2. Les aspirations du client sont l'aspect le plus important de la conception d'une résidence. L'objectif est de dépasser ces aspirations et de créer l'espace au-delà de la propre imagination du client.

3. L'espace de séjour est le centre social de toutes les maisons et ses relations avec les autres espaces sont essentielles. La définition de cet espace englobe tout, même s'il s'agit parfois de l'unique pièce d'un studio.

4. Nous nous éloignons de l'espace minimaliste blanc en employant de plus en plus de couleurs et de textures dans nos projets.

1. Das Haus von John Sloan in London wurde entworfen, um seine große Kunst- und Antiquitätensammlung aufzunehmen. Die Plastizität und Zweideutigkeit der Räume und der Umgang mit dem Tageslicht erhöhen die Architektur auf eine spirituelle Ebene.

2. Die Wünsche des Kunden sind der wichtigste Aspekt beim Entwurf einer Wohnung oder eines Wohnhauses. Ziel des Gestalters ist es, diese Erwartungen noch zu übertreffen und einen Raum zu schaffen, der noch über die Vorstellungskraft des Auftraggebers hinaus geht.

3. Der von allen genutzte Raum ist der soziale Mittelpunkt aller Wohnungen und seine Beziehung zu den übrigen Räumen ist sehr wichtig. Die Definition dieses Raumes bezieht alles mit ein. Manchmal kann es sich dabei um den einzigen Raum in einem Appartement handeln.

4. Wir entfernen uns allmählich von den weißen, minimalistischen Räumen, um im stärkeren Maße wieder Farbe und Textur in unsere Entwürfe einzuführen.

The founders of co-labarchitects worked for many design firms, on both small and large-scale projects, as design architects and design group leaders before establishing co-labarchitects in 2001. Their design approach focuses on responding positively to the client and to the project's environment in order to materialize the aspirations and potential of each. Co-labarchitects feel that it is important to adapt the needs of the client and at the same time take full advantage of the natural characteristics of each location, finding inspiration from various sources to create proposals based on logical analysis.

Les fondateurs de co-labarchitects ont travaillé pour de nombreuses agences, sur des projets à petite et grande échelle, en tant que concepteurs et chefs de projet avant de créer co-labarchitects en 2001. Leur approche conceptuelle se concentre sur la réponse positive à apporter au client et à l'environnement afin de matérialiser aspirations et potentiel. Co-labarchitects pense qu'il est important d'adapter les besoins du client tout en tirant pleinement parti des caractéristiques naturelles de chaque lieu, s'inspirant de différentes sources pour créer des propositions fondées sur une analyse logique.

Die Gründer von co-labarchitects haben bereits für viele Unternehmen im Bereich Innenarchitektur gearbeitet, sowohl in großen als auch in kleinen Projekten. Im Jahre 2001 gründeten sie co-labarchitects. Mit ihren Entwürfen möchten sie die Anforderungen des jeweiligen Kunden und der Umgebung jedes Gebäudes gerecht werden. Für co-labarchitects ist es wichtig, die Bedürfnisse des Kunden zu verstehen und gleichzeitig den Charakter des jeweiligen Ortes als Inspirationsquelle zu nutzen, die man analysiert und als Grundlage der Planung benutzt.

This loft, located in the Flatiron District in the center of New York, was remodeled by the same architect once before in 1990, when it was adapted as a residence and photographic studio. Now with a new family, the client requested another total renovation, this time to turn the entire space into an apartment. The auxiliary spaces like bedrooms, bathrooms, and the television room are laid out around the "great room," which includes the living, dining, and play areas. The kitchen, fully equipped with the latest technology, is at one side of this space. Since most of the windows are located only on the south side of the residence, bright colors and glossy finishes were used to help reflect the natural light in the interior. A glass brick wall that separates the kitchen from a public hallway in the building allows light to flow into the apartment, which becomes a large-scale lamp at night. The materials and finishes used for the interior, like mosaic tiles, maple wood, and natural stone, were chosen for their minimal maintenance requirements.

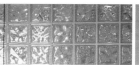    

Flatiron District Loft

Donald Billinkoff Architects

New York, NY, USA, 2003
Photos © Elliott Kaufman Photography

Ce loft, situé dans le quartier de Flatiron, au centre de New York, avait déjà été remodelé en 1990 par le même architecte pour servir d'appartement et de studio de photographie. La nouvelle famille qui l'occupe désirait une rénovation complète afin de transformer cette fois tout l'espace en appartement. Les pièces auxiliaires, comme les chambres, les salles de bains, et le salon de télévision sont aménagées autour de la « grande pièce »,

Dieses Loft im zentral gelegenen Flatiron District in New York wurde 1990 zum ersten Mal von dem Architekten selbst zu einem Fotografiestudio und Wohnung umgebaut. Aufgrund seiner neuen Familie gab der Kunde eine neue Gesamtrenovierung in Auftrag, um sämtliche Räume zu Wohnräumen umzugestalten. Die Nebenräume wie Schlafzimmer, Bäder und der Fernsehraum sind um das "große Zimmer" herum angeordnet, in dem sich Wohn-,

qui comprend la salle de séjour, la salle à manger, et les espaces de jeu. La cuisine, entièrement équipée avec la technologie la plus moderne, occupe un des côtés de cet espace. Comme la plupart des fenêtres sont percées uniquement sur la façade sud de l'appartement, un jeu de couleurs vives et de finitions brillantes permet de renvoyer la lumière naturelle vers l'intérieur. Le mur de pavés de verre qui sépare la cuisine du hall de l'immeuble permet également à la lumière de pénétrer dans l'appartement et se transforme, la nuit, en une grande lampe. Les matériaux utilisés pour la décoration intérieure, comme les carreaux de mosaïque, l'érable et la pierre naturelle, ont été choisis pour l'entretien minimal qu'ils nécessitent.

Ess- und Spielzimmer befindet. Die vollständig mit modernster Technologie ausgestattete Küche liegt neben diesem Raum. Da die meisten Fenster der Wohnung nach Süden liegen, wurden glänzende Farben und Oberflächen gewählt, die das Tageslicht im Inneren widerspiegeln. Eine Wand aus Glasbausteinen trennt die Küche von dem Flur, den alle Gebäudebewohner benutzen. Sie lässt Tageslicht einfallen und wirkt nachts wie eine riesige Lampe. Die im Inneren verwendeten Materialien wie Mosaiken, Ahornholz und Naturstein wurden ausgewählt, weil sie so pflegeleicht sind.

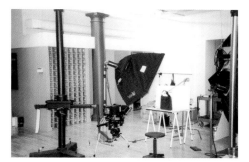

Previous plan

Plan existant

Originalgrundriss

New plan

Plan projeté

Never Grundriss

0   2   4

Sections

Coupes

Schnitte

1. What historical reference in particular inspires you when designing a residence?
Quelles références historiques vous inspirent en particulier lorsque vous dessinez une maison ?
Welche historische Referenz dient Ihnen als Inspiration beim Entwurf eines Hauses?

2. What is the main factor taken into consideration when designing a residence?
Quel facteur principal prenez-vous en considération lors de la conception d'une maison ?
Welche Rahmenbedingungen, bzw. Faktoren sind für Sie ausschlaggebend beim Konzipieren?

3. What room inside the home do you find most interesting to design?
Quelle pièce trouvez-vous la plus intéressante à dessiner ?
Welchen Raum des Hauses finden Sie am spannendsten zu entwerfen?

4. What is your criteria for choosing materials and finishings in a particular room?
Sur quels critères choisissez-vous les matériaux et les finitions d'une pièce ?
Welche Kriterien wenden Sie bei der Entscheidung über Materialien und Oberflächen in diesem Raum an?

1. Our goal is appropriateness: for the site, for the client, for the budget. Of course, our primary interest is contemporary architecture, but we often use evocative materials and colors if they are appropriate.

2. We begin the design process by looking at the site, primarily access and natural light. With an idea of how best to use the site, we then look at the functional organization of the home: flow, adjacencies, program, etc. As the plan begins to develop, we start our investigation of the massing and building form.

3. I can't say there is one particular room we find more interesting than others.

4. Our preference is for contemporary design; simple detailing. But we also prefer that our homes be warm and habitable.

1. Notre objectif est la pertinence : pour le site, le client, le budget. Naturellement, notre principal intérêt est l'architecture contemporaine, mais nous utilisons souvent des matériaux et des couleurs évoquant d'autres époques lorsqu'ils sont appropriés.

2. Nous entamons le processus de conception en observant le site, son accès principal et son éclairage naturel. Ayant une idée de la manière d'utiliser au mieux les lieux, nous étudions alors l'organisation fonctionnelle de la maison : distribution, programme, etc. Nous étudions ensuite la forme structurelle de l'édifice à mesure que le plan se développe.

3. Il n'y a pas de pièce que nous jugions plus intéressante qu'une autre.

4. Notre préférence va à un design contemporain, aux détails simples, mais il nous plaît que nos appartements soient chaleureux et habitables.

1. Unser Ziel ist es, dass alles stimmt, für den Standort, für den Kunden, für das Budget. Unser Hauptinteresse gilt der zeitgenössischen Architektur, aber natürlich benutzen wir auch manchmal Materialien und Farben, die auf andere Epochen anspielen, wenn es in den Kontext passt.

2. Wir beginnen die Planung eines Bauvorhabens mit einer Studie des Grundstücks, wobei wir hauptsächlich den Zugang und die Lichtverhältnisse betrachten. So entsteht zunächst eine Idee, wie man den Ort maximal ausnutzen kann. Dann beginnen wir, an die funktionelle Organisation des Wohnhauses zu denken, die Verteilung, die Wohnfunktionen usw. In dem Maße, in dem der Plan weiter entwickelt wird, fangen wir an, uns über die Form des Gebäudes Gedanken zu machen.

3. Es gibt keinen Raum, den wir interessanter als die übrigen Räume finden.

4. Wir bevorzugen modernes Design mit einfachen Einzelheiten, aber wir möchten warme und wohnliche Räume schaffen.

Donald Billinkoff Architects is an architecture and interior design firm based in New York and founded in 1992. It specializes in the design of residential, commercial, and institutional projects in the New York, New Jersey, Connecticut, and Pennsylvania areas. Their projects, the new construction as well as the renovations, have been featured in many international magazines.

Donald Billinkoff Architects est une agence d'architecture et de décoration intérieures créée en 1992 à New York. Elle est spécialisée dans la décoration de projets résidentiels, commerciaux et institutionnels à New York, dans le New Jersey, le Connecticut et la Pennsylvanie. Leurs projets, qu'il s'agisse de construction nouvelle ou de rénovation, ont été publiés dans nombre de magazines internationaux.

Donald Billinkoff Architects ist ein Büro für Architektur und Innenarchitektur in New York, das 1992 gegründet wurde. Hauptsächlich werden hier Wohn- und Geschäftshäuser und Gebäude für Institutionen in den Regionen New York, New Jersey, Connecticut und Pennsylvania geplant. Sowohl die Neu- als auch die Umbauten dieses Architekten wurden in zahlreichen internationalen Zeitschriften vorgestellt.

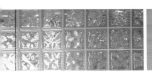

This loft is located on the twelfth floor of a commercial building in New York's Soho neighborhood, and it functions as a permanent design laboratory where materials, models, and prototypes are incorporated into the construction details of the loft. A great variety of materials are used to stimulate the senses, and the various rooms are easily accessible, much like the quarters in a sailboat. The flexibility of the interior is primarily achieved with the furniture, which was especially designed by the architect herself. The flexibility of the furniture and the many ways it can be arranged allow the space to be used as a residence, architectural office, exhibit space, or for entertaining. The space is organized into three main bodies: a central one used as a living room or exhibit space; another one where the kitchen and the meeting space is located; and finally, the bedroom or most private studio. The larger than normal doors, including one in the kitchen that is made of glass, encourage the integration between the different areas.

Flexible Loft

Page Goolrick Architect

New York, NY, USA, 2000
Photos © John M. Hall

Ce loft occupe le douzième étage d'un immeuble commercial du quartier de Soho, à New York, et sert de laboratoire de design permanent où matériaux, modèles et prototypes viennent s'intégrer aux détails de construction du loft. Une grande variété de matières est utilisée pour stimuler les sens, et les différentes pièces sont facilement accessibles, un peu comme les compartiments d'un voilier. La polyvalence de l'espace inté-

Dieses Loft befindet sich im zwölften Stockwerk eines Geschäftshauses in Soho in New York. Es stellt eine Art permanentes Labor für Design dar, in dem Materialien, Modelle und Prototypen sich in die Konstruktionselemente des Lofts selbst einfügen. Man verwendete eine Vielzahl von Materialien, um die Sinne anzuregen. Gleichzeitig sind alle Zimmer im Inneren leicht zu erreichen, so als ob man sich in einem Segelschiff

rieur est essentiellement due au mobilier, spécialement dessiné par l'architecte lui-même. Cette flexibilité du mobilier et les nombreuses manières dont il peut être aménagé permettent d'utiliser le volume aussi bien comme résidence, bureau d'architecture qu'espace d'exposition ou de spectacle. L'espace s'organise en trois corps principaux : celui du centre sert de salle de séjour ou d'espace d'exposition ; un autre est occupé par la cuisine et une salle de réunion ; le troisième, enfin, accueille une chambre ou un atelier privé. Les portes, d'une largeur inhabituelle – notamment celle de la cuisine, réalisée en verre – facilitent l'intégration entre les différents espaces.

befände. Die Flexibilität des Inneren wird hauptsächlich durch die Möbel erreicht, die vom gleichen Architekten entworfen wurden. Die Beweglichkeit der Möbel und die verschiedenen Gestaltungsmöglichkeiten lassen es zu, dass dieser Raum als Wohnung, Architekturbüro, Ausstellungssaal oder Übungsraum benutzt werden kann. Der Raum ist in drei Hauptbereiche unterteilt, ein Zentralteil, der als Wohnzimmer oder Ausstellungsraum dient, ein weiterer Bereich, in dem sich die Küche, die gleichzeitig der Konferenzsaal ist, befindet, und ein Zimmer, das als privates Studio dient. Die großen Türen und die gläserne Küchentür ermöglichen die bessere Integration der verschiedenen Räumlichkeiten.

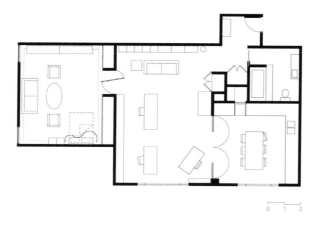

Plan
Plan
Grundriss

1. What historical reference in particular inspires you when designing a residence?
Quelles références historiques vous inspirent en particulier lorsque vous dessinez une maison ?
Welche historische Referenz dient Ihnen als Inspiration beim Entwurf eines Hauses?

2. What is the main factor taken into consideration when designing a residence?
Quel facteur principal prenez-vous en considération lors de la conception d'une maison ?
Welche Rahmenbedingungen, bzw. Faktoren sind für Sie ausschlaggebend beim Konzipieren?

3. What room inside the home do you find most interesting to design?
Quelle pièce trouvez-vous la plus intéressante à dessiner ?
Welchen Raum des Hauses finden Sie am spannendsten zu entwerfen?

4. What is your criteria for choosing materials and finishings in a particular room?
Sur quels critères choisissez-vous les matériaux et les finitions d'une pièce ?
Welche Kriterien wenden Sie bei der Entscheidung über Materialien und Oberflächen in diesem Raum an?

1. Case study houses of the forties and fifties as they had open plans, an emphasis on natural light, efficient use of space and the economical use of simple materials.

2. The site, light, views, and natural ventilation are celebrated and maximized whether we are working on an urban loft or a freestanding structure in a rural context.

3. The hub, or the most heavily used space where the family comes together and where they socialize with others. The hub may be the living room, a family room or what is often referred to as the great room where all the social activities overlap.

4. Functionality, beauty, ease of maintenance, texture, durability. We like to show clients new ways to use materials they are familiar with.

1. Les maisons typiques des années 1940 et 1950, avec leurs plans ouverts, l'accent mis sur la lumière naturelle, l'utilisation efficace de l'espace et l'emploi raisonné des matériaux.

2. Le lieu, la lumière, les vues et la ventilation sont toujours mis en avant, que nous travaillions sur un loft urbain ou une maison individuelle dans un contexte rural.

3. Le lieu central ou l'espace le plus utilisé, celui où la famille se rassemble et se socialise. Ce lieu peut être la salle de séjour, une pièce de famille ou ce que l'on appelle la grande pièce, là où toutes les activités sociales se recouvrent.

4. Fonctionnalité, beauté, entretien facile, texture, durabilité, et le désir de présenter différemment à nos clients des matériaux auxquels ils sont habitués.

1. Die typischen Häuser aus den Vierziger und Fünfzigerjahren mit ihren offenen Stockwerken, die Bedeutung des Tageslichts, die effiziente Nutzung der Räume und die Sparsamkeit beim Einsatz von Materialien.

2. Der Standort, das Licht, die Aussicht und die natürliche Lüftung sind in jedem unserer Bauvorhaben wichtig. Das gilt sowohl für die Fabriketage in der Stadt als auch für ein einzeln stehendes Gebäude in einer ländlichen Umgebung.

3. Das Zentrum oder der meistbenutzte Raum, in dem sich die Familie trifft oder in dem sie Gäste empfängt. Dieser Ort kann das Wohnzimmer sein, ein Familienzimmer oder manchmal ein großer Raum, in dem sich alle sozialen Aktivitäten überschneiden.

4. Funktionalität, Schönheit, einfache Pflege, Textur, Haltbarkeit und der Wunsch, den Kunden einen neuen Umgang mit den Materialien zu zeigen.

Page Goolrick Architect is an architecture and interior design firm based in New York since 1988. The firm's team operates under the shared belief that design excellence results from a simple, clear, and rational attitude, which will create structures that are suitable for our own time period as well as for each specific context and project. The firm's goal is to be able to simplify everyday functions, and in that way fulfill the varied interests and spatial requirements of each client.

Page Goolrick Architect est une agence d'architecture et de décoration intérieure basée à New York depuis 1988. L'équipe qui la compose partage l'idée que l'excellence en design résulte d'une attitude simple, claire et rationnelle, capable de créer des structures convenant à notre époque comme à chaque contexte et projet spécifiques. L'objectif de l'agence est de pouvoir simplifier les fonctions quotidiennes et, de cette manière, satisfaire les différents intérêts et besoins d'espace de chaque client.

Page Goolrick Architect ist ein Architekturbüro, das seit 1988 in New York tätig ist. Dieses Architektenteam folgt der Devise, dass man ein ausgezeichnetes Design durch eine einfache, klare und rationale Haltung erreicht, um so Strukturen zu schaffen, die für unsere spezifische Zeit geeignet sind, und zwar für jeden Zweck und Kontext. Ziel des Büros ist es, die täglichen Funktionen zu vereinfachen und so den verschiedenen Interessen jedes Kunden gerecht zu werden und Räume für alle Bedürfnisse zu schaffen.

The Sempacher building, located in a desirable residential area of Zurich, is an excellent example of modern and sustainable urban restoration. The lot was occupied by a monotonous apartment block from the 1930's that urgently needed to be brought up to date. A detailed preliminary study showed that everything from the electrical installations to the plumbing needed to be upgraded, but that the structure itself would not permit any improvements in the quality of the spaces. A decision was made to replace the building with a new one that would incorporate three main characteristics: a flexible structure that would allow future generations to make changes; a modern building that would maintain a harmonious dialogue with the surrounding structures; and a structure that was sensitive to its environment, taking into account the life cycles of its materials. The spaces have a utility core where the kitchens and bathrooms are located, allowing the living quarters to be more flexible. The building is covered with overlapping translucent pieces that protect it from the sun. Both the color and the texture created by this shell help the building fit into its urban surroundings.

Sempacher Apartments

Camenzind Evolution

Zurich, Switzerland, 2002
Photos © Camenzind Evolution

Le Sempacher Building, situé dans un quartier résidentiel couru de Zurich, est un excellent exemple d'une restauration urbaine moderne et respectueuse de l'environnement. Le terrain était occupé par un immeuble d'appartements sans cachet des années 1930 qui avait d'urgence besoin d'une rénovation. Une étude préliminaire minutieuse avait indiqué qu'il fallait tout refaire, depuis l'installation électrique jusqu'à la plomberie, mais

Das Sempacher-Haus, das in einer gepflegten Wohngegend in Zürich liegt, ist ein ausgezeichnetes Beispiel für die moderne und umweltfreundliche Restaurierung eines Stadtgebäudes. Auf dem Grundstück befand sich ein eintöniger, renovierungsbedürftiger Wohnblock aus den Dreißigerjahren. Die vorherige Gebäudeanalyse ergab, dass das gesamte Gebäude einschließlich elektrischer und sanitärer Installationen modernisiert werden musste,

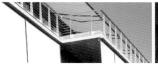

que l'état de la structure ne permettrait pas d'améliorer la qualité des espaces. La décision fut prise de remplacer le bâtiment par un nouvel immeuble qui aurait trois caractéristiques principales : une structure souple permettant aux générations futures de la modifier ; un immeuble moderne qui établirait un dialogue harmonieux avec le bâti environnant ; et une structure sensible à l'environnement, tenant compte des cycles de vie des matériaux employés. Les appartements présentent un noyau utilitaire où sont aménagées les cuisines et salles de bains, offrant ainsi plus de flexibilité aux pièces de séjour. Le bâtiment est couvert de plaques translucides à clin qui le protègent du soleil. La couleur et la texture que crée cette enveloppe participent à l'intégration de l'immeuble dans son environnement urbain.

dass aber die Struktur selbst keine Verbesserung der Qualität der Räume zuließ. So entschied man sich für einen Abriss und einen Neubau, der folgende Eigenschaften haben sollte: eine flexible Struktur, die Veränderungen für künftige Generationen erlaubt, ein modernes Gebäude, das sich harmonisch in die Umgebung einfügt und eine umweltgerechte Bauweise unter Berücksichtigung der Lebensdauer der Materialien. Küchen und Bäder befinden sich alle im gleichen Bereich, so dass die Wohnräume flexibler gestaltet werden konnten. Das Gebäude besitzt eine lichtdurchlässige, sich überlappende Verkleidung, die vor direkter Sonne schützt. Sowohl die Farbe als auch die Textur dieser Verkleidung tragen dazu bei, dass sich das Gebäude perfekt in seine Umgebung einfügt.

Ground floor
Rez-de-chaussée
Erdgeschoss

0 3 6

First floor
Premier étage
Erster Stock

Second floor
Deuxième étage
Zweiter Stock

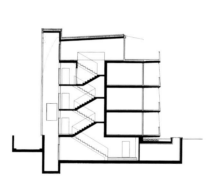

Sections
Coupes
Schnitte

Elevations
Élévations
Aufrisse

1. What historical reference in particular inspires you when designing a residence?
   Quelles références historiques vous inspirent en particulier lorsque vous dessinez une maison ?
   Welche historische Referenz dient Ihnen als Inspiration beim Entwurf eines Hauses?

2. What is the main factor taken into consideration when designing a residence?
   Quel facteur principal prenez-vous en considération lors de la conception d'une maison ?
   Welche Rahmenbedingungen, bzw. Faktoren sind für Sie ausschlaggebend beim Konzipieren?

3. What room inside the home do you find most interesting to design?
   Quelle pièce trouvez-vous la plus intéressante à dessiner ?
   Welchen Raum des Hauses finden Sie am spannendsten zu entwerfen?

4. What is your criteria for choosing materials and finishings in a particular room?
   Sur quels critères choisissez-vous les matériaux et les finitions d'une pièce ?
   Welche Kriterien wenden Sie bei der Entscheidung über Materialien und Oberflächen in diesem Raum an?

1. Our experiences have taught us the importance of local events and microstructures. Especially important to our work is the respect of people's local identity and roots.

2. Architecture is in most cases not the staging of the special, but the design of the common. Like our clothes, buildings must not only fulfil practical, but also emotional requirements. We are not interested in designing just technically perfect buildings that have no 'emotional responders' and therefore feel cold and dead to the user.

3. It's never one room but always the movement between rooms, which creates the space and the emotional experience within it.

4. Materials, finishes and color are some of the many ingredients of architecture. But we see these ingredients more as an 'enhancer' of conceptions or emotional intentions.

1. Notre expérience nous a appris l'importance des circonstances concrètes et des microstructures. L'identité des personnes et leurs racines sont particulièrement importantes dans notre travail.

2. L'architecture n'est pas, la plupart du temps, une mise en scène de quelque chose de spécial, mais la conception de l'ordinaire. Comme nos vêtements, les bâtiments ne doivent pas uniquement satisfaire à des besoins pratiques mais également émotionnels. Cela ne nous intéresse pas de concevoir des bâtiments parfaits qui n'offrent pas de « réponse émotionnelle » et semblent donc froids pour leurs occupants.

3. Il n'y a jamais une seule pièce mais toujours ce mouvement entre les pièces, qui crée à l'intérieur l'espace et l'expérience émotionnelle.

4. Matériaux, finitions et couleurs sont quelques-uns des nombreux ingrédients de l'architecture, mais ce sont des éléments qui renforcent des concepts et non des intentions émotionnelles.

1. Unsere Erfahrungen haben uns die Bedeutung punktueller Umstände und von Mikrostrukturen gelehrt. Die Identität von Personen und ihre Wurzeln sind besonders wichtig für unsere Arbeit.

2. Die Architektur ist in den meisten Fällen nicht der Schauplatz des Besonderen, sondern die Gestaltung des Gewöhnlichen. Wie unsere Kleidung sollten auch Gebäude nicht nur praktische Anforderungen erfüllen, sondern auch emotionale. Es interessiert uns nicht, technisch perfekte Gebäude zu entwerfen, die keine Gefühle wach rufen und auf den Benutzer kalt wirken.

3. Es ist nicht ein Raum, sondern die Bewegung zwischen den Räumen, was den Raum und die emotionale Erfahrung innerhalb des Raumes schafft.

4. Die Materialien, Oberflächen und Farben sind nur einige der vielen Zutaten der Architektur, aber sie sind die Elemente, die die emotionalen Konzepte oder Absichten verstärken.

Architects Stefan Camenzind and Michael Grafensteiner, winners of the Young Architect of the Year Award and the International Design Prize, have firmly positioned themselves among the new generation of notable architects. Their work stands out for its fusion of ingenuity and typical Swiss quality. Stefan Camenzind and Michael Grafensteiner founded their own studio in 1995, after having gained experience working in architectural offices in London, Paris, and Los Angeles. At present they have more than 15 architects practicing with them.

Les architectes Stefan Camenzind et Michael Grafensteiner, lauréats du Young Architect of the Year Award et de l'International Design Prize, appartiennent à la nouvelle génération des architectes de renom. Leur œuvre se démarque par son mélange d'ingéniosité et de qualité typiquement suisse. Stefan Camenzind et Michael Grafensteiner ont créé leur propre agence en 1995, après avoir fait leurs armes à Londres, Paris et Los Angeles. Aujourd'hui, plus de 15 architectes travaillent pour eux.

Die Architekten Stefan Camenzind und Michael Grafensteiner, Preisträger des Young Architect of the Year-Preises und des International Design Award, gehören mittlerweile zur neuen Generation berühmter Architekten. Ihre Arbeit ist vor allem von der Vermischung von Naivität mit der für die Schweiz so typischen Qualität gekennzeichnet. Nachdem sie bereits für Architekturbüros in London, Paris und Los Angeles gearbeitet hatten, gründeten Stefan Camenzind und Michael Grafensteiner 1995 ihr eigenes Studio, in dem gegenwärtig 15 Architekten zusammenarbeiten.

The first step in renovating this loft was to eliminate as many interior walls as possible in order to create a greater feeling of space and light. Very light and flexible materials and design elements were used to fulfill the requirements of the project while preserving the proportions of the space that had been created. The guest room, for example, consists of a foldout bed and two curtains that define the space. The close collaboration of the architects, Roger Hirsch and Miriam Corti, and the interior design team Tocar Inc., was vital in creating the clean and striking atmosphere they were striving for. Materials such as ebony wood, sheer curtains, and Peruvian ceramics created a very elegant and sophisticated atmosphere. The choice of furniture was inspired by the clientís extensive collection of art and photographs in which lively, intense colors are dominant. A palette of soft colors and earth tones was chosen, as well as a few pieces of furniture that would have great impact on the space.

Loft in Tribeca

Roger Hirsch, Myriam Corti + Tocar Inc.

New York, NY, USA, 2002
Photos © Michael Moran

La première étape de la rénovation de ce loft a consisté à éliminer le plus de cloisons possible afin d'augmenter l'impression d'espace et de lumière. On y a ensuite utilisé des matériaux et des éléments décoratifs très légers et flexibles pour satisfaire aux nécessités du projet tout en préservant les proportions du volume ainsi créé. La chambre d'amis, par exemple, se compose d'un lit pliant et de deux rideaux qui définis-

Der erste Schritt bei der Renovierung dieses Lofts bestand in der Beseitigung möglichst vieler Innenwände, um den Eindruck von mehr Raum und Licht zu gewinnen. Um die Proportionen des neu geschaffenen Raums zu wahren, aber gleichzeitig alle notwendigen Wohnräume zu schaffen, wurden sehr leichte und flexible Materialien und Elemente verwendet. Das Gästezimmer zum Beispiel besteht aus einem Klappbett und zwei Gardinen, die den

sent l'espace. L'étroite collaboration entre les architectes Roger Hirsch et Myriam Corti et l'équipe de décoration intérieure de Tocar Inc. a été vitale pour la création de l'atmosphère nette et frappante qu'ils recherchaient. L'ébène, les rideaux de voile et les céramiques péruviennes participent à cette ambiance très élégante et sophistiquée. Le choix du mobilier, restreint mais d'un grand impact, et la palette de couleurs douces et dans les tons terre ont été dictés par la vaste collection d'art et de photographie où dominent les couleurs vives et intenses.

Raum definieren. Die enge Zusammenarbeit der Architekten Roger Hirsch und Myriam Corti mit dem Innenarchitektenteam Tocar Inc trug entscheidend dazu bei, die gewünschte klare und ansprechende Atmosphäre zu schaffen. Materialien wie Ebenholz, die feinen Gardinen und Keramik aus Peru schaffen eine sehr gepflegte Atmosphäre. Die Auswahl der Möbel wurde von der umfassenden Kunst- und Fotografiesammlung der Kunden beeinflusst, in denen lebendige und intensive Farben dominieren. Deshalb wurden die Räumlichkeiten in sanften Farben und Erdtönen gestaltet, mit wenig Möbelstücken, die den Raum jedoch entscheidend gestalten.

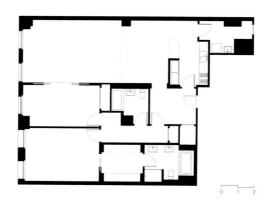

Previous plan

Plan existant

Originalgrundriss

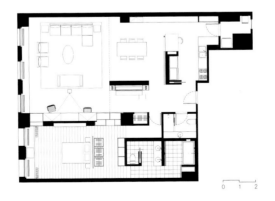

New plan

Plan projeté

Neuer Grundriss

1. What historical reference in particular inspires you when designing a residence?
   Quelles références historiques vous inspirent en particulier lorsque vous dessinez une maison ?
   Welche historische Referenz dient Ihnen als Inspiration beim Entwurf eines Hauses?

2. What is the main factor taken into consideration when designing a residence?
   Quel facteur principal prenez-vous en considération lors de la conception d'une maison ?
   Welche Rahmenbedingungen, bzw. Faktoren sind für Sie ausschlaggebend beim Konzipieren?

3. What room inside the home do you find most interesting to design?
   Quelle pièce trouvez-vous la plus intéressante à dessiner ?
   Welchen Raum des Hauses finden Sie am spannendsten zu entwerfen?

4. What is your criteria for choosing materials and finishings in a particular room?
   Sur quels critères choisissez-vous les matériaux et les finitions d'une pièce ?
   Welche Kriterien wenden Sie bei der Entscheidung über Materialien und Oberflächen in diesem Raum an?

1. We are influenced by classic modernist architects and by artists whose work inspires us.

2. The main starting points for us are the existing context, whether it be a loft interior or a wooded site for a house, and the functional needs of the clients. Our goal is to take these given perameters and then transform them into something that transcends the purely functional.

3. What is most important to us is the interconnection of rooms and how one room flows to the next. In terms of individual spaces, we like to design rooms that present specific design challenges and require inventive solutions.

4. We choose our materials based on the character of a particular room. We like to bring color and texture to surfaces through the use of natural materials.

1. Nous sommes influencés par les architectes modernes classiques et par des artistes dont le travail nous inspire.

2. Les points de départs les plus importants sont le cadre, qu'il s'agisse de l'intérieur d'un loft ou d'un environnement boisé pour une maison, et les besoins fonctionnels du client. Notre objectif est de traduire ces paramètres en quelque chose qui transcende le purement fonctionnel.

3. Le plus important pour nous, c'est l'interconnexion entre les pièces et comment une pièce interfère sur la suivante. En termes d'espaces individuels, nous aimons concevoir des pièces qui présentent des défis de décoration spécifiques et demandent des solutions inventives.

4. Nous choisissons nos matériaux en fonction du caractère d'une pièce spécifique. Nous aimons apporter de la couleur et de la texture aux surfaces par l'emploi de matières naturelles.

1. Wir sind von den klassischen modernen Architekten und von Künstlern, deren Arbeit uns inspiriert, beeinflusst.

2. Die wichtigsten Ausgangspunkte für uns sind der Kontext, egal, ob es sich um das Innere einer Fabriketage oder ein Waldgrundstück für ein Haus handelt, und die funktionellen Bedürfnisse jedes Kundens. Unser Ziel ist es, diese Parameter zu erkennen und in etwas umzuformen, was das rein Funktionelle übersteigt.

3. Für uns ist die Verbindung zwischen den Räumen, und wie ein Raum zum nächsten hin fließt, am wichtigsten. Was die individuellen Räume betrifft, so genießen wir es, Räume zu gestalten, die eine besondere Herausforderung darstellen und neue Lösungen brauchen.

4. Wir wählen die Materialien entsprechend des Charakters jedes einzelnen Raumes aus. Wir bringen gerne mithilfe von natürlichen Materialien Farbe und Textur auf die Wände.

Roger Hirsch Architect (Roger Hirsch y Miryam Corti) is a design firm that specializes in residential and commercial projects. Over the past twelve years its activities have focused on specific clients and locations, resulting in innovative and functional solutions. The firm has received two awards from the Institute of American Architects (AIA) for its residential and retail store designs.
The interior design firm, Tocar, Inc., consists of Susan Vendar and Christina Sullivan. Their design proposals offer a fresh approach to the concept of elegance, mixing classic and contemporary elements.

Roger Hirsch Architect (Roger Hirsch et Myriam Corti) est une agence de design spécialisée dans les projets résidentiels et commerciaux. Au cours des douze dernières années, ses activités se sont concentrées sur des clients et des sites spécifiques, avec des solutions innovantes et fonctionnelles. L'agence a reçu deux récompenses de l'Institute of American Architects (AIA). L'agence de décoration intérieure Tocar Inc. se compose de Susan Vendar et Christina Sullivan. Leurs propositions, où se mélangent éléments classiques et contemporains, offrent une approche nouvelle du concept d'élégance.

Roger Hirsch Architect (Roger Hirsch und Miryam Corti) entwirft vor allem Wohn-, Büro- und Geschäftshäuser. In den letzten zwölf Jahren konzentrierte sich das Büro besonders auf funktionelle und innovative Bauten. Dem Büro wurden zwei Preise vom American Institute of Architects (AIA) für seine Wohn- und Geschäftshäuser verliehen. Tocar, Inc., das Innenarchitekturbüro, wird von Susan Vendar und Christina Sullivan geführt. Ihre Gestaltungsvorschläge nähern sich auf erfrischende Art dem Konzept der Eleganz an, indem klassische und zeitgenössische Elemente gemischt werden.

This interior, originally a six-room apartment in the center of Vienna, was converted into an open loft-style space for living and working. All the interior walls were demolished and the separation between the bathroom, the kitchen, and the bedroom was created with a single, red wall. The idea was to create two zones, one near the interior patio, where the single-function rooms are located – like the bathroom, the kitchen, and the bedroom – and another area facing the street containing a large multifunctional room where several activities can be carried out. The changeable character of this space depends on who is using it and what activities are taking place in it. An effort was made to ensure that the materials and the finishes of certain furnishings were related to the style of the original space. The kitchen table was made of concrete and covered with a natural resin. The bathroom floor is white mosaic tile, while linoleum was used in the rest of the private areas of the home. The original parquet was preserved, as were many of the building's original decorative details.

Small Loft in Vienna

Lakonis Architekten

Vienna, Austria, 2002
Photos © Margherita Spiluttini

Cet intérieur, à l'origine un appartement de six pièces situé dans le centre de Vienne (Autriche), a été converti en un espace de type loft pour y vivre et travailler. Toutes les cloisons intérieures ont été retirées et un simple mur rouge sépare la salle de bains, la cuisine et la chambre. L'idée était de créer deux zones, l'une proche du patio intérieur, où sont situées les pièces à fonction unique – comme la salle de bains, la cuisine et la

Eine ehemalige Sechszimmerwohnung im Zentrum von Wien wurde in ein offenes Loft zum Leben und Arbeiten umgebaut. Alle Innenwände wurden abgerissen und das Bad, die Küche und das Schlafzimmer durch eine einzige rote Wand abgetrennt. Es sollten zwei Zonen geschaffen werden, eine zum Innenhof, wo sich die Räume mit einer einzigen Funktion befinden, wie das Bad, die Küche und das Schlafzimmer, während die andere Zone, in der sich

chambre – et l'autre, sur rue, abritant une grande pièce polyvalente, dont le caractère changeant dépend de qui l'utilise et des activités qui y ont lieu. Un effort a été fait pour que la matière et les finitions de certains meubles soient liées au style de l'espace originel. La table de cuisine a été réalisée en béton et couverte de résine naturelle. Le sol de la salle de bains est en carreaux de mosaïque blancs, tandis que celui des pièces privées de l'appartement est couvert de linoléum. Le parquet original a été conservé, tout comme de nombreux détails décoratifs originels de l'immeuble.

ein großer, multifunktioneller Raum für diverse Aktivitäten befindet, zur Straße liegt. Der wechselnde Charakter dieses Raums hängt von den Bewohnern und deren Aktivitäten in diesem Raum ab. Mit ausgewählten Materialien und bestimmten Möbeln wurde versucht, eine Beziehung zum einstigen Stil der Räume aufrecht zu erhalten. Der Küchentisch ist aus mit Naturharz beschichtetem Beton. Das Badezimmer ist mit weißem Mosaik gefliest, während die übrigen Privaträume Linoleumböden haben. Im vorderen Teil des Hauses wurden das Originalparkett und viele dekorative Elemente des Originalgebäudes beibehalten.

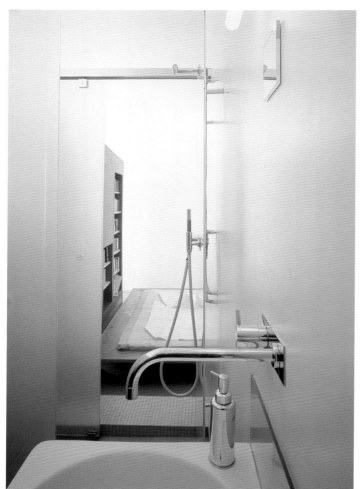

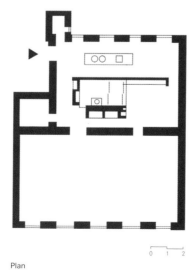

Plan

Plan

Grundriss

1. What historical reference in particular inspires you when designing a residence?
Quelles références historiques vous inspirent en particulier lorsque vous dessinez une maison ?
Welche historische Referenz dient Ihnen als Inspiration beim Entwurf eines Hauses?

2. What is the main factor taken into consideration when designing a residence?
Quel facteur principal prenez-vous en considération lors de la conception d'une maison ?
Welche Rahmenbedingungen, bzw. Faktoren sind für Sie ausschlaggebend beim Konzipieren?

3. What room inside the home do you find most interesting to design?
Quelle pièce trouvez-vous la plus intéressante à dessiner ?
Welchen Raum des Hauses finden Sie am spannendsten zu entwerfen?

4. What is your criteria for choosing materials and finishings in a particular room?
Sur quels critères choisissez-vous les matériaux et les finitions d'une pièce ?
Welche Kriterien wenden Sie bei der Entscheidung über Materialien und Oberflächen in diesem Raum an?

1. Buildings which invite us to use them in a new way: that can be large rooms like lofts in old factories as well as small rooms like the houses of Adolf Loos in Vienna.

2. To give people not only comfort, that is anyway important, but also to make them keen on discovering something new, like children in a barn.

3. It depends on how open the client is, so we are able to change the terms of each room.

4. The effect of materials depends on the way they are used. The unusual combination of well-known materials is often the way to spark people's interest.

1. Les bâtiments qui nous invitent à habiter sur un mode différent : il peut s'agir de vastes espaces comme un loft aménagé dans une ancienne usine ou de petits appartements comme dans les maisons d'Adolf Loos à Vienne.

2. Offrir aux gens non seulement du confort, c'est certes important, mais également leur donner l'envie de découvrir quelque chose de nouveau, comme des enfants dans une grange.

3. Nous pouvons modifier la destination de chaque pièce en fonction de l'ouverture d'esprit du client.

4. L'effet des matériaux dépend de la manière dont ils sont employés. La combinaison inhabituelle de matériaux connus est souvent un moyen d'éveiller l'intérêt des gens.

1. Gebäude, die uns dazu einladen, sie anders zu benutzen, können große Räume im Stile der alter Fabriketagen oder kleine Räume wie in den Häusern von Adolf Loos in Wien sein.

2. Den Menschen soll nicht nur Komfort geboten werden, was sehr wichtig ist, sondern es soll auch eine Neugierde in ihnen geweckt werden, etwas Neues zu entdecken, so wie bei Kindern auf einem Bauernhof.

3. Je nachdem, wie offen der Kunde ist, sind wir dazu in der Lage, die Situation in jedem Raum zu ändern.

4. Die Wirkung der Materialien hängt davon ab, wie sie benutzt werden. Die ungewöhnliche Kombination von gut bekannten Materialien ist oft eine Form, um das Interesse der Menschen zu erwecken.

Mira Thal (Innsbruck, Austria, 1964) and Michael Buchleitner (Stuttgart, Germany, 1959) joined to found the architectural office of Lakonis Architekten in Vienna, in 1995. For them architecture is directly related to man's perception of the natural world, as well as being connected to the makeup of our cultural identity. In this sense, architecture fulfills both functional and economic requirements, by offering universal solutions for our environment. The firm offers a wide range of services, design, construction management, organization and budget management, in all phases of the project.

Mira Thal (Innsbruck, Autriche, 1964) et Michael Buchleitner (Stuttgart, Allemagne, 1959) se sont associés en 1995 pour créer l'agence Lakonis Architekten à Vienne (Autriche). Pour eux, l'architecture est directement liée à la perception qu'a l'homme du monde naturel mais aussi à la formation de notre identité culturelle. En ce sens, l'architecture satisfait à la fois des exigences fonctionnelles et économiques en offrant des solutions universelles pour notre environnement. L'agence propose une gamme étendue de services : conception, gestion de chantier, organisation et gestion de budget.

Mira Thal (Innsbruck, Österreich, 1964) und Michael Buchleitner (Stuttgart, Deutschland, 1959) gründeten im Jahr 1995 in Wien das Architekturbüro Lakonis Architekten. Für die beiden Architekten steht die Architektur in direkter Verbindung mit unserer Wahrnehmung der Welt und der Gestaltung unserer kulturellen Identität. Deshalb gibt die Architektur Antworten auf funktionelle und ökonomische Anforderungen, um globale Lösungen für unsere Umgebung zu bieten. Das Architekturbüro bietet umfassende Dienstleistungen, über Entwurf und Bauleitung bis hin zur Kostenüberwachung, Organisation und Überwachung aller Projektphasen.

This is the first phase, designed by the architects, for the transformation of the old Lords Telephone Exchange offices, in the center of London. The original structure of the building was ideal for creating urban living spaces on multiple levels, resulting in a project for 36 residential units, including 5 penthouses, which occupy the entire top floor of the building. The architects, in collaboration with Philippe Starck, were awarded the commission for the design and construction of this complex in a competition. This resulted in the creation of a series of unique, modern apartments, with fine details and finishes, within a plan that made the most of the structural and lighting conditions that already existed. Each living unit was based on the same concept: the creation of a unique and ample space for the living areas and independent areas for the kitchen, bedroom, and bathroom. A large variety of interiors were created in the eleven floors that make up the building, enriched by the changes in level, high ceilings, and exterior terraces.

Lords Telephone Exchange

Paskin Kyriakides Sands

London, UK, 2002
Photos © Paskin Kyriakides Sands

Voici la première phase de la transformation d'un ancien immeuble de bureaux du Lords Telephone Exchange, situé dans le centre de Londres. La structure originelle du bâtiment était idéale pour créer des espaces de vie urbains sur plusieurs niveaux et offrir 36 appartements, dont 5 penthouses occupant tout le dernier étage de l'immeuble. Les architectes, en collaboration avec Philippe Starck, remportèrent le concours pour la

Es handelt sich um die erste Phase der Umgestaltung des Unternehmens Lords Telephone Exchange im Herzen von London. Die Originalstruktur des Gebäudes eignet sich ausgezeichnet zur Schaffung von Stadtwohnungen auf verschiedenen Stockwerken. So wurden 36 Wohnungen geplant, zu denen 5 Dachwohnungen gehören, die den gesamten oberen Stock des Gebäudes einnehmen. Die Architekten gewannen die Ausschreibungen

conception et la construction de cette résidence. Il en résulte un ensemble d'appartements de style unique et moderne, avec de beaux détails et finitions, à l'intérieur d'un plan qui s'appuie le plus possible sur la structure et les conditions d'éclairage existantes. Chaque unité d'habitation s'appuie sur le même concept : la création d'un vaste et unique volume pour les séjours et des zones indépendantes pour la cuisine, la chambre et la salle de bains. Des intérieurs très divers, enrichis par des modifications de niveau, des hauts plafonds et des terrasses extérieures, ont ainsi été créés sur les onze étages.

für die Gestaltung und den Bau dieses Wohnkomplexes. Dabei wurden sie von Philippe Starck unterstützt. Durch die Planung entstanden eine Reihe von modernen und einzigartigen Wohnungen mit schönen Details und interessanter Gestaltung. Insgesamt wurde aus der vorhandenen Struktur und dem Licht der größtmögliche Nutzen gezogen. Jede Wohneinheit ging von dem gleichen Konzept aus. Man wollte einen einzigen und weiten Raum für das Wohnzimmer und unabhängige Bereiche für die Küche, das Schlafzimmer und das Bad schaffen. In den elf Stockwerken des Gebäudes entstanden sehr vielfältige Wohnungen, die durch verschiedene Ebenen, doppelte Höhe oder Terrassen bereichert werden.

0   3   6

General plans

Plans d'ensemble

Generalgrundrisse

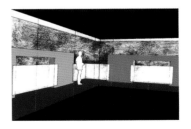

0 1 2

Plan
Plan
Grundriss

Elevations
Élévations
Aufrisse

Interior view
Vue intérieure
Innenansicht

Paskin Kyriakides Sands is a London firm founded in 1974 by Douglas Paskin, and it has grown to become a nationally known company thanks to the recognition received for its work. The firm specializes in urban planning, from modest new construction jobs to large urban renewal projects and master plans. Their main emphasis is the integration of the project into its surroundings, and strategic plans. They have vast experience in residential design, from luxury units to large apartment complexes.

Paskin Kyriakides Sands est une agence londonienne fondée en 1974 par Douglas Paskin, qui a acquis progressivement une certaine notoriété en Grande-Bretagne. L'agence est spécialisée dans le planning urbain, depuis la réalisation de modestes constructions nouvelles jusqu'à de grands projets de rénovation et des plans maîtres. Leur principal objectif est l'intégration du projet dans son environnement et la planification stratégique. Ils ont une vaste expérience dans la conception de résidences, qu'il s'agisse d'appartements de luxe ou de grands immeubles d'habitation.

Paskin Kyriakides Sands ist ein Unternehmen, das 1974 von Douglas Paskin in London gegründet wurde. Die Firma gewann durch ihre bekannten Projekte internationale Anerkennung. Das Unternehmen hat sich auf Stadtplanung spezialisiert, wobei sowohl Neubauten als auch große Renovierungsprojekte und Masterpläne durchgeführt werden. Die Unternehmensphilosophie basiert auf der Integration der Bauten in ihren Kontext und in die Stadtplanung. Man blickt auf eine langjährige Erfahrung im Bau von Wohnungen und Wohnhäusern zurück, angefangen bei luxuriösen Villen bis hin zu großen Wohnkomplexen.

The goal of this project was to convert an old shop on the ground floor of a building into a residence for the interior designer that collaborated with the architects on this project. Since the space was located between shared walls, the manipulation of natural light became the principal aspect of the design. It determined the form, the spatial distribution, and even the color of the project. The two existing façades were completely opened up with large windows that not only let the light into the interior, but also linked it with the exterior. Sliding glass doors separating the centrally located bedrooms and bathroom allow light to enter and fully integrate them with the rest of the house. The pursuit of light is also reflected in the details, finish, and furniture. White is the dominant color in all the areas, and only a few specific pieces of natural wood stand out in this continuous uniform setting. A white façade and a white resin floor complete the picture, resulting in a home that is light and open, and in which the spaces are dynamic participants.

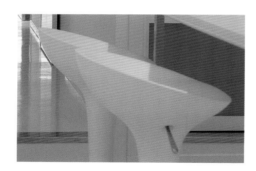

House in the Coast

Joan Estrada / Special Events

Barcelona, Spain, 2003
Photos © Nuria Fuentes

L'objectif était de convertir une vieille boutique située au rez-de-chaussée d'un immeuble en une résidence destinée au décorateur qui collaborait avec les architectes sur ce projet. Le volume étant fermé par des murs mitoyens, le traitement de la lumière naturelle – déterminant la forme, la distribution spatiale et même la couleur du projet – devint l'enjeu principal de la conception. Les deux façades existantes furent entiè-

Es handelt sich um den Umbau eines ehemaligen Lokals in einem Erdgeschoss in eine Wohnung für den Innenarchitekten selbst, wobei die Architektinnen an der Planung mitarbeiteten. Da das Lokal von Zwischenwänden begrenzt wird, war das Tageslicht der wichtigste Faktor für die Planung, der die Form, Verteilung und sogar die Farben bestimmte. Die beiden bereits vorhandenen Fassaden wurden durch weite Fenster vollständig

rement ouvertes par de larges baies qui non seulement ouvrait l'intérieur à l'éclairage naturel mais le reliait également à l'extérieur. Les portes vitrées coulissantes qui séparent les chambres et la salle de bains, aménagées au centre, laissent entrer la lumière tout en intégrant ces pièces au reste de l'appartement. La recherche de luminosité se retrouve également dans les détails, les finitions et le mobilier. Le blanc domine dans toutes les pièces et seuls quelques éléments en bois naturel se détachent de ce cadre uniforme et continu, que complètent une façade blanche et un sol en résine blanc. Il en résulte une maison claire et ouverte, dans laquelle les volumes participent de manière dynamique.

geöffnet, so dass einerseits viel Licht in die Räume dringt und andererseits eine Verbindung nach draußen hergestellt wird. Die wichtigsten Räume der Wohnung, die Schlafzimmer und das Bad werden ebenfalls durch verglaste Schiebetüren abgetrennt, durch die Licht fällt. So werden auch diese Räume in die übrigen Wohnungsbereiche integriert. Diese Suche nach Licht spiegelt sich auch in anderen Einrichtungselementen, Materialien und Möbelstücken wieder. Weiß ist überall die dominierende Farbe, und nur einige besondere Teile aus naturbelassenem Holz heben sich vor diesem einheitlichen und durchgehenden Rahmen ab. Sogar die Fassade und der Boden aus Kunstharz sind weiß. So entstand eine offene und klare Wohnung, in der die Räume dynamisch gestaltet werden können.

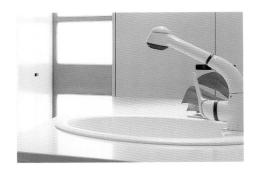

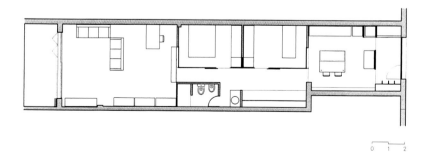

0 1 2

Plan
Plan
Grundriss

This loft is located in a three-story structure built in the late nineteenth century, originally used for the manufacture of dental products. Beginning in the 1940's the building was used for artist's studios. The client's and the architect's original idea was based on creating a living and working environment, experimenting with different lighting, materials, and treatments of the space. The separation between the three different areas: an office, a meeting space, and living quarters was created using vertical expanses similar to trenches. These spaces were devised by removing part of the ironwork between the ground floor and the basement, and constructing an interior mezzanine. In doing so, the materials and characteristics of the industrial building were highlighted and a very dramatic interior space was created. The office and the meeting area, in contrast with the original rustic look of the brick and wood beams, were literally laid out as metallic islands surrounded by water.

Ling Office and Loft

David Ling

New York, NY, USA, 2000
Photos © Reto Guntli / zapaimages

Ce loft est aménagé dans un immeuble de trois étages construit à la fin du XIXe siècle, employé à l'origine pour la fabrication de produits dentaires et transformé au début des années 1940 pour abriter des ateliers d'artistes. Le client et l'architecte avaient l'idée de créer un environnement de vie et de travail en employant différents éclairages, matériaux et modes de traitement de l'espace. La séparation entre les trois différents volumes –

Dieses Loft befindet sich in einem dreistöckigen Gebäude aus dem 19. Jh., das einst als Fabrik für Dentalprodukte errichtet wurde, und in dem sich seit den Vierzigerjahren Kunstateliers befinden. Die Idee des Architekten und des Kunden war es, eine Umgebung zum Leben und Arbeiten zu schaffen, in der mit verschiedenen Materialien, räumlichen Bedingungen und Beleuchtung experimentiert wird. Die Trennung der drei verschiedenen Zonen des

un bureau, une salle de réunion, et un espace d'habitation – a été réalisée grâce à des espaces verticaux semblables à des tranchées, ensuite subdivisés en retirant une partie de la charpente métallique entre le rez-de-chaussée et le sous-sol et en construisant une mezzanine. Cela crée un espace intérieur dramatique tout en mettant en valeur les matériaux et le caractère originel du bâtiment industriel. Le bureau et la salle de réunion, par opposition à l'apparence rustique originelle de la brique et des poutres en bois, ont été littéralement conçus comme des îles métalliques cernées par les eaux.

Gebäudes, Büro, Zusammenkünfte und Wohnen, wurde durch vertikale, grubenähnliche Räume geschaffen. Diese Räume entstanden durch das Entfernen von Teilen des Mauerwerks zwischen dem Erdgeschoss und dem Keller, so dass ein Zwischen-geschoss geschaffen wurde. Damit hob man die Besonderheit und die Materialien dieses Industriegebäudes hervor und es entstand ein sehr dramatisch wirkender Innenraum. Als Gegensatz zu den rustikalen Originalmaterialien wie Ziegelstein und Holzbalken wurden das Büro und das Besprechungszimmer als eine Art von Wasser umgebene metallische Insel gestaltet.

Ground floor

Rez-de-chaussée

Erdgeschoss

0   1   2

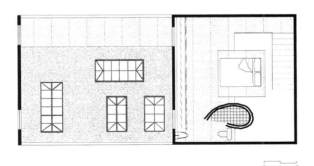

First floor

Premier étage

Erster Stock

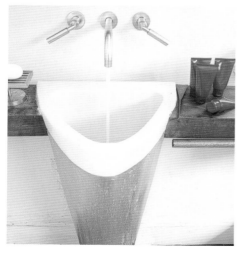

1. What historical reference in particular inspires you when designing a residence?
Quelles références historiques vous inspirent en particulier lorsque vous dessinez une maison ?
Welche historische Referenz dient Ihnen als Inspiration beim Entwurf eines Hauses?

2. What is the main factor taken into consideration when designing a residence?
Quel facteur principal prenez-vous en considération lors de la conception d'une maison ?
Welche Rahmenbedingungen, bzw. Faktoren sind für Sie ausschlaggebend beim Konzipieren?

3. What room inside the home do you find most interesting to design?
Quelle pièce trouvez-vous la plus intéressante à dessiner ?
Welchen Raum des Hauses finden Sie am spannendsten zu entwerfen?

4. What is your criteria for choosing materials and finishings in a particular room?
Sur quels critères choisissez-vous les matériaux et les finitions d'une pièce ?
Welche Kriterien wenden Sie bei der Entscheidung über Materialien und Oberflächen in diesem Raum an?

---

1. Actually I am inspired by sculpture: Richard Serra, Eduardo Chillida, early Giacometti, early Noguchi, Anish Kapoor, Martin Puryear. Among architects I admire early Mies van der Rohe, Le Corbusier, Carlo Scarpa, Pierre Chareau, late Kahn.

2. For me the main factor is the physical idiosyncrasies of the space and the personal idiosyncrasies of the client.

3. I enjoy designing the entertaining space which for me is the kitchen/dining room since I design them together.

4. I like to juxtapose opposite materials and forms. Smooth against hard, rustic against refined.

---

1. Je suis réellement inspiré par la sculpture : Richard Serra, Eduardo Chillida, Anish Kapoor, Martin Puryear, et les premières œuvres de Giacometti et de Noguchi. Parmi les architectes que j'admire, il y a Mies van der Rohe pour ses premières réalisations, Le Corbusier, Carlo Scarpa, Pierre Chareau, et les dernières œuvres de Kahn.

2. Le principal facteur est l'idiosyncrasie de l'espace et de la propre personnalité de chaque client.

3. J'aime dessiner un espace plaisant, comme la cuisine et la salle à manger, que je conçois ensemble.

4. J'aime juxtaposer des matériaux et des formes opposés. Doux contre dur, rustique contre raffiné.

---

1. Ich werde wirklich von der Bildhauerei inspiriert. Richard Serra, Eduardo Chillida, Anish Kapoor, Martin Puryear oder die ersten Arbeiten von Giacometti und Noguchi. Unter den Architekten bin ich ein Bewunderer der ersten Werke von Mies van der Rohe, Le Corbusier, Carlo Scarpa, Pierre Chareau und der letzten Bauten von Kahn.

2. Der wichtigste Faktor ist die Idiosynkrasie des Raumes und die eigene, persönliche jedes Kundens.

3. Ich genieße es, unterhaltsame Räume wie die Küche und das Speisezimmer zu entwerfen, die ich beide zusammen entwerfe.

4. Ich liebe die Nebeneinanderstellung von gegensätzlichen Formen und Farben. Weich gegen stark, rustikal gegen elegant.

David Ling's multicultural background strongly influences his professional career. Brought up in the United States and educated in Europe, Ling still maintains his ties with China. After working as an associate in the offices of Richard Meier and I. M. Pei he established his own architectural office, David Ling Architects, in 1992. Ling defines the essence of his work as an artistic integration of space, form, light, and function enriched with materials. For Ling, all projects present a unique challenge, because of their diverse natures and variety of locations.

Les antécédents multiculturels de David Ling ont fortement influencé sa carrière professionnelle. Élevé aux États-Unis et formé en Europe, Ling n'a jamais rompu ses liens avec la Chine. Après avoir collaboré comme associé avec Richard Meier et I.M. Pei, il a créé sa propre agence d'architecture, David Lings Architects, en 1992. Ling définit l'essence de son travail comme une intégration artistique de l'espace, des formes, de la lumière et de la fonction, qu'enrichissent les matériaux. Pour Ling, chaque projet est un défi unique en raison de sa nature et de la diversité des sites.

Die berufliche Laufbahn von David Ling ist erheblich durch seine multikulturelle Erziehung geprägt. Er wuchs in den Vereinigten Staaten auf, erhielt seine Ausbildung in Europa und ist durch seine Herkunft für immer mit China verbunden. Nachdem er als assoziierter Mitarbeiter im Büro von Richard Meier und I. M. Pei tätig war, gründete er 1992 sein eigenes Architekturbüro David Ling Architects. Er selbst definiert das Wesentliche seiner Arbeit als eine künstlerische Integration von Raum, Form, Licht und Funktion, die durch Gegenständlichkeit bereichert wird. Ling beschäftigt sich mit sehr verschiedenen Projekten und Standorten.

This design project involved transforming an old industrial loft into a residence for a young family. The building, which originally housed a printing company, was recently converted into a residential building. The main goal was to preserve the magnificent views and sources of natural light present when the space was empty, while incorporating all the requirements of the new design. Concrete was poured to level the floor and to insulate it from the lower level acoustically. Walls for defining rooms were kept to a minimum, and a slightly lower false ceiling was added for certain lighting fixtures and to hide the utility installations. The main space of the loft has two central structures containing two bathrooms and a studio, which are covered with light wood and glass that lets light flow into the interiors. The configuration of these two elements defines the spaces and provides privacy where needed, while creating an interesting flow through the interior.

Light Loft

Desai / Chia Architecture

New York, NY, USA, 2004
Photos © Paul Warchol

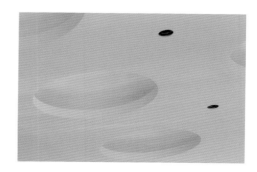

Ce projet consistait en la conversion d'un ancien loft industriel en résidence pour une jeune famille. Le bâtiment, qui abritait autrefois une imprimerie, avait été récemment converti en immeuble d'habitation. L'objectif principal était de conserver les vues magnifiques et les sources de lumière naturelle qu'offrait le volume vide tout en incorporant les éléments nécessaires au nouvel aménagement. Une chape de béton a permis de sur-

Hier wurde eine ehemalige Fabriketage in eine Wohnung für eine junge Familie umgestaltet. Das Gebäude, in dem sich einst eine Druckerei befand, wurde komplett zu einem Wohnblock umgebaut. Hauptziel der Planung war es, den wundervollen Blick und die guten Lichtverhältnisse des leeren Gebäudes auszunutzen, aber dennoch alle für ein komfortables Wohnen notwendigen Räumlichkeiten zu schaffen. Es wurde ein durchgehen-

élever le sol et de l'isoler acoustiquement du niveau inférieur. Les cloisons définissant les pièces ont été réduites au minimum, et un faux-plafond bas et léger a été ajouté pour les éclairages et pour dissimuler les circuits d'eau et d'électricité. Le volume principal du loft présente deux structures centrales contenant deux salles de bains et un bureau recouverts d'un léger lattis de bois et de verre qui laisse pénétrer la lumière à l'intérieur. La configuration de ces deux éléments définit les espaces et fournit l'intimité nécessaire à ces pièces tout en créant un parcours intéressant dans l'appartement.

der Betonfußboden über den alten Boden gelegt, um die Höhenunterschiede auszugleichen. Dieser diente gleichzeitig als Geräuschdämmung für die darunter liegenden Stockwerke. Es wurde versucht, so wenig Wände wie möglich zur Begrenzung der einzelnen Räume zu schaffen, und es wurde eine etwas tiefere, doppelte Decke eingezogen, die die Installationen für die Beleuchtung, Elektrizität und sanitären Anlagen verdeckt. Der allgemeine Raum das Lofts besteht aus zwei zentralen Körpern, in denen sich zwei Bäder und ein Atelier befinden, und die von einer leichten Haut aus Holz und Glas umgeben sind, durch die das Licht in das Innere dringt. Die Anordnung dieser beiden Körper ermöglicht eine Gesamtwahrnehmung des Raumes, aber gleichzeitig werden die Räumlichkeiten begrenzt und in bestimmten Zonen die Privatsphäre geschützt. So entstand eine interessante innere Struktur.

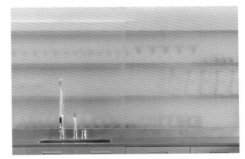

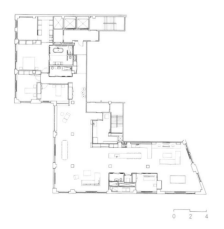
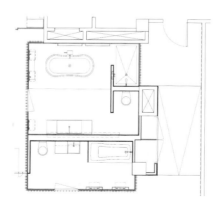
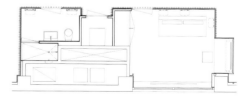

0   2   4

0   1   2

General plan

Plan général

Generalgrundriss

Bathroom area plans

Plans des salles de bains

Badezimmergrundrisse

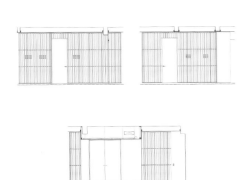

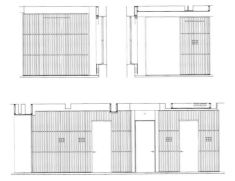

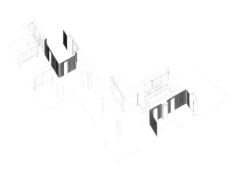

Interior elevations

Élévations intérieures

Innenaufrisse

Axonometry

Axonométrie

Axonometrie

Desai / Chia Architecture was founded in 1995 by Catherine Chia and Arjun Desai in New York City. The architectural style of the firm is based on simplicity and an emphasis on the careful and articulated use of light and materials. Special attention is given to the roles of space and form in the design and function of each project. The firm is not given to excessive conceptualization; rather, it sees architecture as a field where tradition, innovation, and imagination should be present in proper measure.

L'agence Desai/Chia Architecture a été créée à New York en 1995 par Catherine Chia et Arjun Desai. Leur style architectural s'appuie sur la simplicité et l'accent mis sur l'utilisation minutieuse de la lumière et des matériaux et leur articulation. Ils prêtent une attention particulière aux rôles de l'espace et de la forme dans la conception et la fonction de chaque projet. L'agence ne cherche pas une conceptualisation excessive, mais voit l'architecture comme un domaine où la tradition, l'innovation, et l'imagination doivent être présents dans leur juste mesure.

Desai / Chia Architecture wurde 1995 von Catherine Chia und Arjun Desai in New York gegründet. Das Unternehmen sucht mit seiner Architektur die Einfachheit, wobei besonderer Nachdruck auf den intelligenten Gebrauch des Lichtes und der Materialien gelegt wird. Bei allen Wohnfunktionen und auch der Gesamtfunktion jedes einzelnen Gebäudes werden Form und Raum berücksichtigt. Das Unternehmen versucht, nicht den Weg der übertriebenen Konzeptualität einzuschlagen, sondern seine Architektur als ein Handwerk aufzufassen, in dem die Tradition, die Innovation und die Phantasie in der richtigen Menge vorhanden sind.

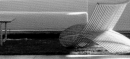

This project was a renovation of a loft in an old industrial building north of Tribeca, very near the Hudson River. The residence is on the third floor and has wonderful views of the river, which is dramatically different on weekdays than on the weekend. The long and narrow space had large windows on the west side and other smaller windows on the east side. The main objective of the renovation project was to reinforce the effect of the panorama and to take full advantage of the natural light in the interior. The flexibility and control of the natural light is achieved with 24 sliding glass panels. The combined living room, studio, and guest area was placed at the rear of the space, to enjoy the best lit area of the residence. Each one of these settings can be compartmentalized to form a separate unit, or joined into a single common space. Reflective materials, like steel and glass, direct the light to the least illuminated part of the residence, where the most private areas, the bedroom and the bathroom, are located.

DeBenedetto / Jiang Loft

Smith and Thompson Architects

New York, NY, USA, 2001
Photos © Doug Baz

Ce projet concernait la rénovation d'un loft, au troisième étage d'un ancien bâtiment industriel au nord de Tribeca, tout près de l'Hudson. L'appartement dispose de vues magnifiques sur le fleuve, dont l'aspect est très différent en semaine et le week-end. Le volume, long et étroit, est ouvert par de grandes baies sur sa façade ouest et d'autres fenêtres plus petites sur le côté est. L'objectif principal était d'accentuer l'effet du panorama

Die Planung besteht in der Renovierung eines Lofts in einem ehemaligen Industriegebäude im Norden von Tribeca ganz in der Nähe des Flusses Hudson River. Die Wohnung befindet sich in einem zweiten Stock und man genießt von ihr aus einen wundervollen Blick auf den Fluss, eine Landschaft, die sich an Wochentagen und am Wochenende ganz anders präsentiert. Es handelt sich um einen langen und engen Raum, der große Fenster nach

et de tirer le meilleur parti de l'éclairage naturel. Cette luminosité, contrôlée et réglable, est obtenue par 24 panneaux vitrés coulissants. L'ensemble salle de séjour, bureau et chambre d'amis a été placé sur l'arrière pour profiter de la partie la mieux éclairée de l'appartement. Chacune de ces zones peut être compartimentée pour former une unité séparée, ou être réunie en un seul espace commun. Des matériaux réfléchissants, comme l'acier et le verre, dirigent la lumière vers la partie la plus sombre de l'appartement, où sont aménagées les pièces les plus intimes, comme la chambre et la salle de bains.

Westen und kleine nach Osten hatte. Das Hauptziel der Renovierung war es, den wundervollen Blick noch zu verbessern und das Tageslicht soweit wie möglich auszunutzen. Die Flexibilität und die Kontrolle des Lichtes erreichte man durch 24 verschiebbare Paneele aus Glas. Die Gruppe Wohnzimmer, Atelier und Gästezimmer liegt hinten im Raum, wo auch das meiste Tageslicht einfällt. Jede dieser Zonen kann unterteilt werden, so dass eine getrennte Einheit entsteht, oder mit den anderen zu einem einzigen Raum vereinigt werden. Reflektierende Materialien wie Stahl und Glas leiten das Licht in den weniger hellen Teil der Wohnung weiter, in dem sich die privateren Räume wie das Schlafzimmer und das Bad befinden.

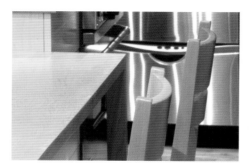

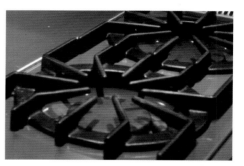

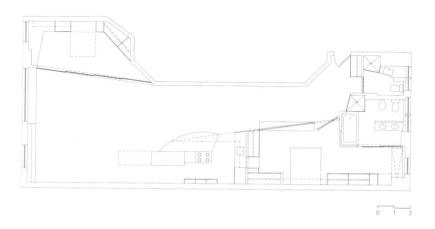

Plan
Plan
Grundriss

1. What historical reference in particular inspires you when designing a residence?
Quelles références historiques vous inspirent en particulier lorsque vous dessinez une maison ?
Welche historische Referenz dient Ihnen als Inspiration beim Entwurf eines Hauses?

2. What is the main factor taken into consideration when designing a residence?
Quel facteur principal prenez-vous en considération lors de la conception d'une maison ?
Welche Rahmenbedingungen, bzw. Faktoren sind für Sie ausschlaggebend beim Konzipieren?

3. What room inside the home do you find most interesting to design?
Quelle pièce trouvez-vous la plus intéressante à dessiner ?
Welchen Raum des Hauses finden Sie am spannendsten zu entwerfen?

4. What is your criteria for choosing materials and finishings in a particular room?
Sur quels critères choisissez-vous les matériaux et les finitions d'une pièce ?
Welche Kriterien wenden Sie bei der Entscheidung über Materialien und Oberflächen in diesem Raum an?

1. We try to bring the sum of our travels and experience to each project; also the particular local history and the vernacular are important to us. One of our recurring favorite historical references is Fatepur Sikra in Rajasthan, India. It seems relevant to all scales and types of projects.

2. Interpreting a client's program is the first creative step in a design. We then think of these ideas in relationship to the specific site.

3. Those spaces that share multiple functions as well as connector spaces between specific rooms.

4. Light and continuity.

1. Nous essayons d'enrichir chacun de nos projets de la somme de nos voyages et de notre expérience ; mais l'histoire locale et le folklore sont également importants pour nous. Une de nos références historiques favorites est Fatepur Sikra, dans le Rajasthan, en Inde. Ce monument semble s'accorder à toutes les échelles et à tous les types de projets.

2. La première étape créative de la conception est l'interprétation du programme du client. Nous reprenons ensuite ces idées en relation avec le site spécifique.

3. Les espaces polyvalents ainsi que les espaces reliant des pièces déterminées.

4. La lumière et la continuité.

1. Wir versuchen, die Summe unserer Reisen und Erfahrungen in jede Planung einzubringen. Ebenso wichtig ist für uns die jeweilige Geschichte und volkstümliche Kultur. Eine unserer liebsten historischen Referenzen ist Fatepur Sikra, in Rajasthan in Indien. Sie scheint für jede Art und Größenordnung der Planung eine Rolle zu spielen.

2. Der erste kreative Schritt für die Gestaltung ist die Interpretation der Bedürfnisse des Kunden. Anschließend denken wir an diese Ideen im Zusammenhang mit dem spezifischen Standort.

3. Die Räume, die mehreren Funktionen dienen und die Räume, die verschiedene Zimmer miteinander verbinden.

4. Das Licht und die Kontinuität.

Smith and Thompson Architects is an architectural firm that was founded by G. Phillip Smith and Douglas Thompson in 1975 in New York. The office mainly designs residences, institutions, and commercial interiors. In 1989 they won a competition to do the construction of the East Hampton airport. They earned the Beaux Arch award for the design of the Kleeb residence, and the AIA Award for the design of the Jacques Marchais Tibetan Art Museum.

Smith and Thompson Architects est une agence d'architecture fondée en 1975 à New York par G. Phillip Smith et Douglas Thompson. L'agence conçoit essentiellement des résidences, des institutions, et des intérieurs de boutiques. En 1989, elle a remporté le concours pour la construction de l'aéroport de East Hampton, ainsi que le Beaux Arch Award pour la résidence Kleeb, et le AIA Award pour la conception du musée d'art tibétain Jacques Marchais.

Smith and Thompson Architects wurde 1975 von G. Phillip Smith und Douglas Thompson in New York gegründet. Das Unternehmen plant hauptsächlich Wohnungen und Wohnhäuser, Gebäude für Institutionen und Geschäftsräume. 1989 gewann es die Ausschreibung für die Errichtung des Flughafens von East Hampton und ihm wurden mehrere Preise wie der Beaux Arch Award für die Gestaltung des Wohnhauses Kleeb und der AIA Award für die Gestaltung des Museum for Tibetan Art Jacques Marchais verliehen.

The challenge of this project consisted of transforming the structure of a rather small late nineteenth century industrial building, into a one-room residence that could also be used as a photo studio. Because of the small amount of usable space the approach consisted of keeping the intervention to a minimum, using only the pieces necessary for resolving the design, and preserving the original character of the space as much as possible. Recycled panels, which contain the electricity and water installations, were used to cover the floor with a raised platform, mirroring the original surface and acting as an insulating space for the length of the room. Two small areas were created, one for the bathroom and the other for laundry and storage. The placement of these two settings serves to divide the entire space into all its functional parts. The original details of the building were preserved whenever possible, and they stand out as an integral part of the interior design. Hand tools were used to help achieve the desired look in every case, for example, the refurbishing of the columns and beams and in the treatment of the exposed brick walls.

   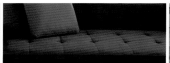 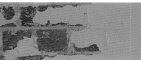

TB Guest Loft

Tom McCallum, Shania Shegedyn

Melbourne, Australia, 2003
Photos © Shania Shegedyn

Le défi de ce projet consistait à transformer la structure d'un assez petit bâtiment industriel de la fin du XIXᵉ siècle en un appartement d'une pièce pouvant également être utilisé comme studio de photographie. En raison du faible volume utilisable, l'approche choisie a consisté à intervenir au minimum en n'utilisant que les éléments nécessaires à la décoration, et à préserver le plus possible le caractère originel de l'espace. Des

Die Herausforderung bei dieser Planung bestand darin, die Struktur eines kleinen ehemaligen Fabrikgebäudes vom Ende des 19. Jh. in eine Wohnung mit einem Raum umzuformen, der gleichzeitig als Fotostudio benutzt werden konnte. Da kaum Platz da war, wurden so wenig Eingriffe wie möglich durchgeführt, und nur die notwendigen, funktionellen Elemente eingeführt, so dass der Originalcharakter der Räumlichkeiten weitgehend erhalten

panneaux recyclés posés sur le sol créent une sorte de faux-plancher, qui évoque la surface d'origine et, agissant comme isolant, dissimule les circuits électriques et d'eau. Deux petits espaces accueillent pour l'un la salle de bains, pour l'autre la laverie et une buanderie. La disposition de ces deux pièces permet de diviser l'espace en ses parties fonctionnelles. Les détails originaux du bâtiment, conservés chaque fois que possible, s'intègrent remarquablement dans la décoration intérieure. Pour obtenir l'effet désiré, la rénovation des colonnes et des poutres et le traitement des murs de briques apparentes, entre autres, ont été réalisés avec un outillage à main.

blieb. Mit wiederverwerteten Holzplatten wurde ein Podium auf dem Fußboden gebaut. So wurde der Originalboden nachempfunden und gleichzeitig entstand eine Isolierschicht über dem ganzen Raum, durch die man die elektrischen und hydraulischen Installationen führen konnte. Es wurden zwei kleine Räume geschaffen, einer dient als Bad und der andere als Wasch- und Lagerraum. Diese beiden Räume sind so angeordnet, dass sie den gesamten Raum in seine funktionellen Bereiche unterteilen. Die Originalelemente des Gebäudes wurden so weit wie möglich erhalten und in die Innengestaltung miteinbezogen. Bei all diesen Arbeiten wie die Restaurierung der Säulen und Dachbalken und die Behandlung der Wände aus unverputztem Ziegelstein wurden handwerkliche Techniken benutzt, durch die man das gewünschte Aussehen erzielte.

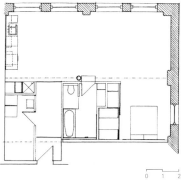

Plan
Plan
Grundriss

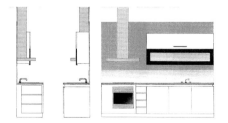

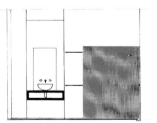

Interior elevations

Élévations intérieures

Innenaufrisse

1. What historical reference in particular inspires you when designing a residence?
   Quelles références historiques vous inspirent en particulier lorsque vous dessinez une maison ?
   Welche historische Referenz dient Ihnen als Inspiration beim Entwurf eines Hauses?

2. What is the main factor taken into consideration when designing a residence?
   Quel facteur principal prenez-vous en considération lors de la conception d'une maison ?
   Welche Rahmenbedingungen, bzw. Faktoren sind für Sie ausschlaggebend beim Konzipieren?

3. What room inside the home do you find most interesting to design?
   Quelle pièce trouvez-vous la plus intéressante à dessiner ?
   Welchen Raum des Hauses finden Sie am spannendsten zu entwerfen?

4. What is your criteria for choosing materials and finishings in a particular room?
   Sur quels critères choisissez-vous les matériaux et les finitions d'une pièce ?
   Welche Kriterien wenden Sie bei der Entscheidung über Materialien und Oberflächen in diesem Raum an?

---

1. There is no historic reference in particular; however, I employ a modernist design sensibility.

2. The main factor taken into consideration when designing a residence is respect to the original environment and pared back design where every single room is ergonomic, energy efficient and aesthetically beautiful to be in.

3. The bathroom.

4. A minimal and natural color palette which mirrors finishes throughout the interior. In this case bluestone.

---

1. Je n'ai pas de références historiques particulières, bien que j'ai une sensibilité décorative moderniste.

2. Le facteur le plus important que je prends en considération lors de la conception d'un appartement est de respecter l'environnement original et de créer une décoration minimale où toutes les pièces sont ergonomiques, énergiquement efficaces et esthétiquement agréables.

3. La salle de bains.

4. Une gamme de couleurs minimale et naturelle qui met en valeur les finitions.

---

1. Keine historische Referenz im Besonderen, obwohl ich mich auf das Konzept des modernistischen Designs beziehe.

2. Der wichtigste Faktor, der beim Entwurf einer Wohnung oder eines Hauses beachtet werden muss, ist der Respekt für die ursprüngliche Umgebung und die Schaffung eines minimalen Designs, in dem alle Räume ergonomisch und energetisch wirksam und ästhetisch angenehm sind.

3. Das Bad.

4. Eine minimale und natürliche Farbpalette, die Gestaltungselemente im ganzen Inneren unterstreicht.

The philosophy of the Tom McCallum design firm is to condense the practice into an essential search for beauty, ergonomics, and energy efficiency. To achieve a design that flows harmoniously, a systematic method is employed in every project, first analyzing the characteristics of the site, and later introducing the functional aspects. The design is always conditioned more by the ergonomic solutions for the use of the space than by decisions based on esthetics. Natural colors complement this Minimalist approach. This results in interiors that look spacious, that are easy to use, pleasing to touch, and visually calm.

La philosophie de l'agence de décoration Tom McCallum est de concentrer la pratique dans une recherche essentielle de la beauté, de l'ergonomie et de l'efficacité énergétique. La recherche d'une décoration harmonieuse s'effectue pour chaque projet grâce à une méthodologie systématique, où sont d'abord analysés les caractéristiques du site puis ses aspects fonctionnels. Le décor est davantage conditionné par les solutions ergonomiques d'utilisation de l'espace que par des décisions esthétiques. Cette approche minimaliste est enrichie par des couleurs naturelles, qui donnent un intérieur spacieux, facile à vivre visuellement paisible.

Die Philosophie des Designbüros Tom McCallum verbindet die Aspekte Schönheit, Ergonomie und Ökonomie. Für die harmonische Gestaltung ihrer jeweiligen Projekte werden zunächst die Umstände jedes Ortes systematisch analysiert, dann werden die funktionellen Aspekte eingeführt. Deshalb unterliegt die Gestaltung immer den ergonomischen Aspekten der Benutzung des Ortes, aber sie basiert auch auf ästhetischen Gesichtspunkten. Natürliche Farben ergänzen das minimalistische Design. So entstehen leicht zu nutzende Räume, die weiträumig wirken, einladend sind und eine visuelle Ruhe ausstrahlen.

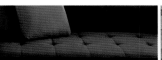

This loft, located in the middle of New York's popular Soho neighborhood, is home to a couple and their two small children. Despite the clients' desire to live in an industrial space in the center of the city, when faced with designing the space with the help of the architects they discovered several features that were inherited from previous conventional home layouts. Instead of creating an austere, white cube, they designed a space with more classical orders and sophisticated decoration. The result created a strong contrast between the existing architecture and the interior design. The layout of the residence is simple and easy to read: a central space, with dramatic windows illuminating the interior, contains the living and dining areas. A space partially divided by glass doors houses the kitchen while the two guest bedrooms are more independently located at the eastern side. The master bedroom, at one end of the residence, enjoys more privacy since it is separated from the central space by several very large shelves. Original architectural elements, like the columns, the system of beams, and the metal partitions on the façade, were emphasized in the space.

Loft in Soho

Ziba Khalili, Alexandr Neratoff

New York, NY, USA, 2002
Photos © Marina Berio, Jean Christian Bourcart

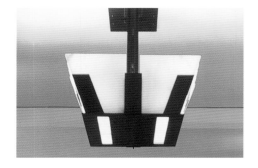

Ce loft, situé au centre de Soho, un quartier populaire de New York, abrite un couple et ses deux enfants. Alors qu'ils souhaitaient vivre dans un espace industriel au centre de la ville, ils se sont rendus compte, au moment de réaliser la décoration avec les architectes, qu'ils devaient tenir compte de nombre d'éléments hérités de leur ancienne résidence, plus conventionnelle. Aussi, au lieu de créer un cube austère et blanc, conçurent-ils un

Mitten im berühmten Viertel Soho in New York liegt dieses Loft, in dem ein Paar mit seinen kleinen Kindern lebt. Auch wenn sie den Wunsch hegten, in einer Fabriketage mitten in der Stadt zu leben, entdeckten sie, während sie zusammen mit den Architekten den Raum planten, dass sie zahlreiche Bedürfnisse aus ihren vorherigen, konventionellen Wohnungen einzubringen hatten. So entstanden aus diesen Räumlichkeiten anstelle eines weißen, nüch-

volume d'ordre plus classique et montrant une décoration sophistiquée. Il en résulte un fort contraste entre l'architecture existante et la décoration intérieure. Le plan de l'appartement est simple et facile à lire : un espace central, dont les fenêtres éclairent l'intérieur, accueille la pièce de séjour et la salle à manger. Un volume partiellement divisé par des portes vitrées abrite la cuisine tandis que les deux chambres d'amis, indépendantes, occupent le côté est. La chambre principale, à une extrémité de l'appartement, jouit de plus d'intimité, étant séparée de l'espace central par plusieurs grandes bibliothèques. Les éléments architecturaux d'origine, comme les colonnes, la poutraison et les cloisons métalliques en façade, ont été mises en valeur.

ternen Würfels klassischere Räume mit einer edlen Dekoration. Dies führte zu einem starken Kontrast zwischen der existierenden Architektur und der Raumgestaltung. Ein anderer Raum, der teilweise durch Glastüren unterteilt ist, beherbergt die Küche, und die Gästezimmer liegen etwas unabhängiger im östlichen Bereich. Der wichtigste Raum auf einer Seite der Wohnung wirkt etwas privater, da er durch große Regale von dem zentralen Teil abgetrennt ist. Die originalen architektonischen Elemente wie Säulen, Dachbalken und die Unterteilung der Fassade durch Metallelemente wurden erhalten.

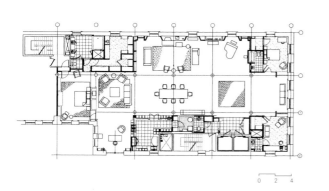

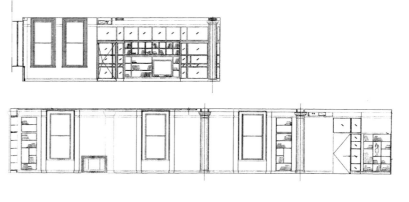

Plan
Plan
Grundriss

Sections
Coupes
Schnitte

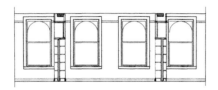

Sections

Coupes

Schnitte

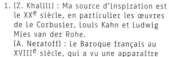

1. What historical reference in particular inspires you when designing a residence?
   Quelles références historiques vous inspirent en particulier lorsque vous dessinez une maison ?
   Welche historische Referenz dient Ihnen als Inspiration beim Entwurf eines Hauses?

2. What is the main factor taken into consideration when designing a residence?
   Quel facteur principal prenez-vous en considération lors de la conception d'une maison ?
   Welche Rahmenbedingungen, bzw. Faktoren sind für Sie ausschlaggebend beim Konzipieren?

3. What room inside the home do you find most interesting to design?
   Quelle pièce trouvez-vous la plus intéressante à dessiner ?
   Welchen Raum des Hauses finden Sie am spannendsten zu entwerfen?

4. What is your criteria for choosing materials and finishings in a particular room?
   Sur quels critères choisissez-vous les matériaux et les finitions d'une pièce ?
   Welche Kriterien wenden Sie bei der Entscheidung über Materialien und Oberflächen in diesem Raum an?

1. [Z. Khalili]: My inspirations are the twentieth century, in particular the works of Le Corbusier, Louis Kahn and Ludwig Mies van der Rohe.
   [A. Neratoff]: The Baroque in France during the 18th century, when a rarely innovation in small scale domestic architecture happened.

2. [Z. Khalili]: Different approaches to designing a house might be taken; nevertheless, the relationship of a house to site remains the main generator of form.
   [A. Neratoff]: The cultural framework, the clients' needs and cultural references, etc.

3. [Z. Khalili]: Any room, which has a mixed used function.
   [A. Neratoff]: Any room that does not work out right away.

4. [Z. Khalili]: They are based on the design concept, function of the room, client preferences and creating a particular mood.
   [A. Neratoff]: Their ability to define the shape of the three-dimensional forms they clad.

1. [Z. Khalili] : Ma source d'inspiration est le XXe siècle, en particulier les œuvres de Le Corbusier, Louis Kahn et Ludwig Mies van der Rohe.
   [A. Neratoff] : Le Baroque français au XVIIIe siècle, qui a vu apparaître une certaine innovation dans l'architecture domestique à petite échelle.

2. [Z. Khalili] : On peut avoir différentes approches pour concevoir une maison, cependant les relations d'une maison au site restent le principal générateur de forme.
   [A. Neratoff] : Le cadre et les références culturels, les besoins du client, etc.

3. [Z. Khalili] : Toute pièce qui a des fonctions mixtes.
   [A. Neratoff] : Toute pièce qui ne se comprend pas de manière évidente.

4. [Z. Khalili] : Ils sont fondés sur le concept de décoration, la fonction de la pièce, les préférences du client et la création d'une ambiance particulière.
   [A. Neratoff] : La capacité des matériaux à définir la forme des volumes tridimensionnels qu'ils habillent.

1. [Z. Khalili]: Meine Inspirationsquelle ist das 20. Jahrhundert, insbesondere die Arbeiten von Le Corbusier, Louis Kahn und Ludwig Mies van der Rohe.
   [A. Neratoff]: Der französische Barock im 18. Jahrhundert, wo es zu einer bedeutenden Innovation in der Architektur von kleineren Wohnhäusern kam.

2. [Z. Khalili]: Man kann an die Gestaltung eines Hauses auf verschiedene Weisen herangehen. Jedoch ist die Beziehung zwischen dem Haus und dem Ort der wichtigste Faktor für die Form.
   [A. Neratoff]: Die kulturellen Rahmenbedingungen, die Ansprüche des Kunden, kulturelle Referenzen...

3. [Z. Khalili]: Jegliches Zimmer mit gemischter Nutzung.
   [A. Neratoff]: Jeglicher Raum, der nicht als solcher verstanden wird.

4. [Z. Khalili]: Es basiert auf dem Konzept der Gestaltung, der Funktion des Raumes, den Vorlieben des Kundens und auf dem Hervorrufen eines besonderen Gemütszustandes.
   [A. Neratoff]: Die Fähigkeit der Materialien, eine dreidimensionale Form zu schaffen, die sie verkleiden.

Ziba Khalili grew up in Iran and pursued her professional education in France. After receiving a Master of Architecture degree, she worked in Paris as an architect for several years. In 1986 she moved to New York where she studied sculpture, winning several prizes for her work. She founded her own architectural firm in 1990 and completed projects in New York and Paris.
Alexandr Neratoff is a native of New York and grew up in the community of Russian immigrants that was formed after the Russian revolution. He received his professional education in the United States.

L'architecte iranienne Ziba Khalili a grandi en Iran et a fait ses études en France. Après avoir obtenu son diplôme, elle a travaillé à Paris comme architecte pendant plusieurs années. En 1986, elle est partie à New York où elle a étudié la sculpture, remportant plusieurs prix pour son œuvre. Elle a créé son agence d'architecture en 1990 et réalisé plusieurs projets à New York et Paris.
Alexandr Neratoff est né à New York et a grandi dans la communauté d'émigrés russes qui s'y était formée après la Révolution russe. Il a fait toutes ses études aux États-Unis.

Die aus dem Iran stammende und dort aufgewachsene Architektin Ziba Khalili absolvierte ihr Studium in Frankreich. Nach dem Studium arbeitete sie mehrere Jahre als Architektin in Paris. 1986 zog sie nach New York um, um sich als Bildhauerin weiterzubilden. Sie gewann mehrere Preise für ihre bildhauerischen Arbeiten. 1990 gründete sie ihr eigenes Architekturbüro und ist seitdem in New York und Paris tätig. Alexandr Neratoff stammt aus New York und wuchs in der Gemeinschaft der russischen Emigranten nach der russischen Revolution auf. Er besuchte die Schule in Frankreich und absolvierte sein Studium in den USA.

This project was designed for a New York couple — one an art critic and the other a movie editor — living in the Hell's Kitchen neighborhood. The residence occupies an entire floor of an old industrial building, and has panoramic views of the city on three sides. The design highlights the industrial context, positioning new elements as if they were sculptures to complement the space and define the layout of the apartment. The result is a box, in which functions like the kitchen and the support areas are consolidated, defining the public and private areas of the loft. The oversize sliding doors that can be opened completely to integrate these areas with the rest of the space are an important element of the design. In general, the color white, the original polished concrete floors, and the exposed utility installations are the predominant elements that emphasize the character of the space. A collection of furniture and decorative elements in wood and soft textiles act as a contrast and create a comfortable environment.

Frank and Amy Loft

Resolution: 4 architecture

New York, NY, USA, 2000
Photos © Reto Guntli / zapaimages

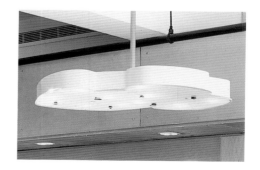

Ce projet a été conçu pour un couple de New-yorkais, un critique d'art et un réalisateur de cinéma. L'appartement occupe tout un étage d'un ancien bâtiment industriel du quartier de Hell's Kitchen, et jouit de vues panoramiques sur la ville sur trois côtés. La décoration met en valeur le contexte industriel en disposant les nouveaux éléments comme des sculptures pour embellir l'espace et définir l'aménagement de l'appar-

Dieser Wohnraum wurde für ein Paar, Kunstkritiker und Cutterin, im Viertel Hell's Kitchen in New York geschaffen. Die Wohnung liegt in einem ehemaligen Industriegebäude und nimmt ein gesamtes Stockwerk ein. Von ihr aus hat man einen wundervollen Blick auf die Stadtlandschaft auf drei Seiten. Die Gestaltung unterstreicht den industriellen Kontext und bringt neue, skulpturelle Elemente ein, die den bereits existierenden Raum ergänzen und Lösungen

   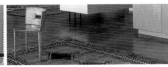 

tement. Il en résulte une boîte dans laquelle sont regroupées les pièces fonctionnelles comme la cuisine et les pièces de service, définissant ainsi les espaces publics et privés du loft. Les grandes portes coulissantes, élément important du décor, peuvent s'ouvrir entièrement pour réintégrer ces pièces à l'ensemble du volume. La couleur blanche, le sol en béton lissé d'origine et les réseaux apparents prédominent et soulignent le caractère particulier de l'espace. Les éléments de mobilier et la décoration en bois et en tissus doux jouent sur les contrastes tout en créant un cadre de vie confortable.

für die Wohnfunktionen schaffen. Als Ergebnis entstand eine Kiste, in der sich die funktionellen Zonen wie die Küche und zusätzlichen Räume konzentrieren, und die die öffentlich und privat genutzten Bereiche des Loftes definiert. Ein wichtiges Element dieser Kiste sind die großen Schiebetüren, die völlig geöffnet werden können, um diese Bereiche in den übrigen Raum zu integrieren. Die im allgemeinen vorherrschende Farbe ist weiß, außerdem wurden die originalen, polierten Betonfußböden, die Fenster und die nicht unter Putz liegenden Installationen beibehalten, was den industriellen Charakter des Raumes unterstreicht. Als Kontrapunkt dient eine Sammlung von dekorativen Möbeln und Elementen aus Holz und weich wirkende Stoffe, die die Räume warm und einladend wirken lassen.

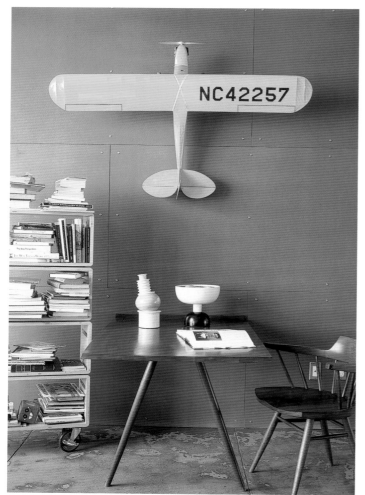

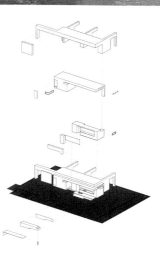

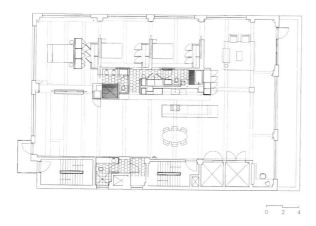

Plan
Plan
Grundriss

Axonometry
Axonométrie
Axonometrie

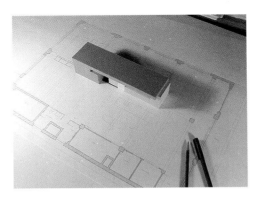

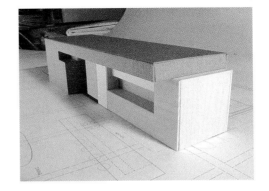

Model
Maquette
Modell

Resolution: 4 architecture is an architectural firm that was founded in 1990 in New York by Joseph Tanney and Robert Luntz. At the present time the company has a team of 10 people who have completed many projects of every size. Their work has earned them several awards including the AIA Award for the design of the offices of an Internet service provider, and a home for the architect Peter Eisenman, as well as the first place award in a contest to design a prefabricated house in Pittsboro.

Resolution: 4 architecture est une agence d'architecture fondée en 1990 à New York par Joseph Tanney et Robert Luntz. Elle compte actuellement 10 personnes et a réalisé de nombreux projets de toutes tailles. L'agence a obtenu plusieurs récompenses, dont le AIA Award pour la conception des bureaux d'un fournisseur de services Internet et pour une maison pour l'architecte Peter Eisenman, ainsi que le premier prix d'un concours pour la conception d'une maison préfabriquée à Pittsboro.

Resolution: 4 architecture ist ein Architekturbüro, das 1990 von Joseph Tanney und Robert Luntz in New York gegründet wurde. Im Augenblick beschäftigt das Unternehmen 10 feste Mitarbeiter und hat bereits zahlreiche Projekte verschiedener Größenordnung durchgeführt. Dem Unternehmen wurden bereits mehrere Preise verliehen, darunter die AIA Awards für die Gestaltung eines Büros für Internetdienstleistungen, ein Preis für ein Wohnhaus für den Architekten Peter Eisenmann und den ersten Platz in einem Wettbewerb für ein Fertighaus in Pittsboro, NC.

This residence is located in an old rope factory in New York. It had to fulfill two functions, those of being a home and also a studio. The interior space demanded a flexible approach to resolve a relatively complex structure. The solution was to create a system of translucent panels that act as dividing elements, shelves, and even as sources of light. These portable units cover the walls in some areas, leaning against the perimeter of the space, or they can be used to define enclosed spaces in the center part of the loft. The lightweight and translucent materials used in their construction allow this flexibility, and the natural light that mainly enters from the north can flow through them. The kitchen cabinets were designed using these same materials, while the kitchen countertop is concrete, cast in place and polished by hand, to match the overall esthetic sense of the residence. The bathroom was designed with an open floor plan, integrated into the rest of the space, with the different fixtures laid out separately. The system of panels allows the space to be adapted according to the requirements of home or work, or to make the interior look different when desired.

Giobbi / Valentino Residence

Bone / Levine Architects

New York, NY, USA, 2002
Photos © Jacek Kucy

Cet appartement, situé dans une ancienne usine de cordage de New York, devait remplir deux fonctions : appartement et bureau. La structure relativement complexe du volume intérieur impliquait l'adoption d'une configuration souple. La solution fut de créer un système de panneaux translucides comme éléments séparatifs, rayonnages, voire sources de lumière. Ces paravents mobiles, en matériaux légers, servent de revêtement

Diese Wohnung befindet sich in einer ehemaligen Kleiderfabrik in New York. Sie dient zwei verschiedenen Zwecken, als Wohnung und als Atelier, wobei zwischen diesen Zonen eine gewisse Flexibilität herrschen sollte, um die recht komplexe Struktur in Griff zu bekommen. Dazu wurde ein System mit durchscheinenden Paneelen entwickelt, die als Raumteilung, Regale und sogar als Lichtquellen dienen. Diese beweglichen Wände werden

mural dans certaines pièces ou, dans la partie centrale du loft, sont employés pour y clore des espaces, sans gêner le passage de la lumière naturelle du côté de la façade nord. Ce système de panneaux permet d'adapter l'espace suivant les besoins – vie de famille ou bureau – ou de modifier l'apparence du loft. Les meubles de cuisine ont été conçus dans ces mêmes matériaux, tandis que la paillasse en béton, coulée sur place et polie à la main, s'accorde à l'esthétique générale de l'appartement. Intégrée dans le volume principal, la salle de bains, dont les différents éléments sont indépendants, est conçue sur un plan ouvert.

als Verkleidung der Wandbereiche einiger Zonen benutzt, oder sie formen geschlossene Räume in den mittleren Teilen des Loft. Die Paneele sind aus leichtem und durchscheinendem Material. Sie sorgen für die gewünschte Beweglichkeit und lassen das Licht, das hauptsächlich aus der Nordrichtung kommt, hindurch. Die Küchenmöbel sind aus dem gleichen Material. Nur die Arbeitsflächen in der Küche sind aus gegossenem, handpoliertem Beton, was gut zur allgemeinen Ästhetik der Wohnung passt. Das Bad wurde als offener, in das gesamte Wohnambiente integrierter Raum angelegt, in dem die verschiedenen Elemente separat vorhanden sind. Durch das Paneelsystem können die Räume an die Funktionen Wohnen und Arbeiten angepasst werden und immer wieder aufs Neue neu gestaltet werden.

Plan
Plan
Grundriss

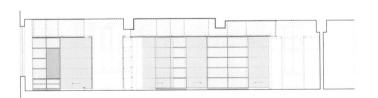
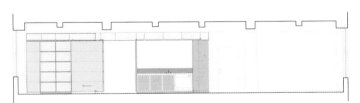

Transversal sections
Coupes transversales
Querschnitt

Kevin Bone and Joseph Levine established their own architecture studio in 1982, with the premise that New York City's constructed environment presents special opportunities, as well as particular problems, for small architecture firms. The firm takes special interest in the materials and construction details that they introduce into their work. The projects strive to be simple, modern, and well constructed, with unexpected combinations of materials and sensitive detailing in their assembly.

Kevin Bone et Joseph Levine ont créé leur agence d'architecture en 1982, convaincus que l'environnement bâti de New York présentait des opportunités particulières, ainsi que des problèmes particuliers, pour les petites agences d'architecture. L'agence s'intéresse particulièrement aux matériaux et aux détails de construction. Les projets s'efforcent d'être simples, modernes et bien construits, avec des combinaisons inédites de matériaux et des détails intéressants dans leur assemblage.

Kevin Bone und Joseph Levine eröffneten ihr eigenes Architekturbüro 1982. Sie waren davon überzeugt, dass sich in der Umgebung von New York für kleine Architekturunternehmen interessante Möglichkeiten ergeben würden, und ganz besondere Probleme zu lösen wären. Die Firma brachte vor allem ihr Interesse an den Materialien und baulichen Details in ihre Arbeit ein. Es wurden einfache, moderne und hochwertige Gebäude errichtet, mit überraschenden Materialkombinationen und interessanten Einzelheiten.

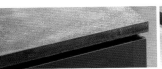

Directory
Cordonnées des architectes
Direktorium

Christoff:Finio architecture
250 West Broadway, 4th floor,
New York, NY 10013, USA
T: +1 212 219 1026
F: +1 212 219 9165
www.christofffinio.com

co-labarchitects
24/28A Hatton Wall,
London EC1N 8JH, UK
T +44 207 242 7255
F +44 207 242 7266
architecture@co-lab.net
www.co-lab.net

Fung + Blatt Architects
104 N. Avenue 56, Suite 3A, Los Angeles,
CA 90042, USA
T: +1 323 255 8368
F: +1 323 255 3646
contact@fungandblatt.com
www.fungandblatt.com

Gabellini Associates
665 Broadway, Suite 706, New York,
NY 10012, USA
T: +1 212 388 1700
F: +1 212 388 1808
www.gabelliniassociates.com

Alden Maddry Architect
928 Lorimer Street, Brooklyn, New York,
NY 11222, USA
T: +1 718 383 1947
am@aldenmaddry.com
www.aldenmaddry.com

Basil Walter Architects
611 Broadway, Suite 311, New York,
NY 10012, USA
T: +1 212 505 1955
F: +1 212 475 7320

Bone / Levine Architects
561 Broadway, 8D, New York,
NY 10012, USA
T: +1 212 219 1038
F: +1 212 226 8056
www.bonelevine.net

Callas Shortridge Architects
3621 Hayden Avenue, Culver City,
CA 90232, USA
T: +1 310 280 0404
F: +1 310 280 0414
mail@callas-shortridge.com
www.callas-shortridge.com

Camenzind Evolution
Samariterstrasse 5, Postfach,
Zurich 8030, Switzerland
T: +41 44 253 9500
F: +41 44 253 9510
info@CamenzindEvolution.com
www.CamenzindEvolution.com

Daniele Claudio Taddei
Feldeggstrasse 54, Zurich 8008,
Switzerland
T: +41 79 409 48 50
taddei@milnor.net

David Ling
225 East 21st Street, New York,
NY 10010, USA
T: +1 212 982 7089
F: +1 212 475 1336
www.davidlingarchitect.com

Delugan_Meissl
Mittersteig 13/4, Vienna 1040, Austria
T: +43 1 585 36 90
F: +43 1 585 36 90-11
haasler@deluganmeissl.at
www.deluganmeissl.at

Desai / Chia Architecture
54 West 21st Street, New York,
NY 10010, USA
T: +1 212 366 9630
F: +1 212 366 9278
www.desaichia.com

Donald Billinkoff Architects
310 Riverside Drive 202-1, New York,
NY 10025, USA
T: +1 212 678 7755
F: +1 212 678 7743
yprokesch@billinkoff.com
www.billinkoff.com

Gregory Phillips Architects
66 Great Cumberland Place,
London W1H 7FD, UK
T: +44 207 724 3040
www.gregoryphillips.com

Guillermo Arias + Luis Cuartas
Carrera 11 84-42, int. 5, Bogotá,
Colombia
T: +57 1 257 9501
garias@octubre.com.co
www.octubre.com.co

Holodeck.at
Friedrichstrasse 6/15,
Vienna 1010, Austria
T: +43 1 524 8133-0
F: +43 1 524 8133-4
vienna@holodeck.at
www.holodeck.at

Insite Architecture Design
20 Rue de Billancourt,
Boulogne 92100, France
T: +33 01 41 10 22 70
F: +33 01 41 10 22 71
www.insitedsign.com

Joan Estrada / Special Events
Vigatans 6, bajos, Barcelona 08003, Spain
T: +34 93 268 8614
F: +34 93 268 8615
joanestrada@joanestrada.com
www.joanestrada.com

John Wardle Architects
Level 10, 180 Rusell Street, Melbourne,
Victoria 3000, Australia
T: +61 3 9654 8700
F: +61 3 6954 8755
johnwardle@johnwardlearchitects.com
www. johnwardlearchitects.com

Jonathan Levi Architects
266 Beacon Street, Boston,
MA 02116, USA
T: +1 617 437 9458
www.leviarc.com

Lakonis Architekten
Rueppgasse 11, Vienna 1020, Austria
T: +43 1 216 0 215
buchleitner.thal@lakonis.at
www.lakonis.at

Leo Frei Architekten
Bergstrasse 50, Stäfa 8712, Switzerland
T: +41 1 926 7401
info@frei-arch.ch
www.frei-arch.ch

Marcio Kogan
Al Tiete, 505, São Paulo, Brasil
T: +55 011 3018 3522
F: +55 011 3063 3424
mk-mk@uol.com.br

Mark Mack Architects
2343 Eastern Court
Venice, CA 90291, USA
T: +1 310 822 0094
F: +1 310 822 0019
office@markmack.com
www.markmack.com

Page Goolrick Architect
20 W 22 Street, Suite 1505, New York,
NY 10010, USA
T: +1 212 219 3666
F: +1 212 414 5768
pg@goolrick.com
www.goolrick.com

Paskin Kyriakides Sands
7 Cliff Road Studios, London NW1 9AN, UK
T: +44 207 424 4800
F: +44 207 424 4801
info@pksarchitects.com
www.pksarchitects.com

Resolution: 4 architecture
150 W, 28th Street, Suite 1902, New York,
NY 10001, USA
T: +1 212 675 9266
info@re4a.com
www.re4a.com

Roger Hirsch, Myriam Corti
91 Crosby Street, New York,
NY 10012, USA
T: +1 212 219 2609
F: +1 212 219 2767
rhirschny@aol.com

Samuel Lerch
Eibenstr. 9, Zurich 8045, Switzerland
T: +41 1 382 4655
samnad@swissonline.ch

Sandra Aparicio + Forteza Carbonell Associats
Marià Aguiló 1-3, local 5,
08005 Barcelona, Spain
T: +34 93 307 6501
F: +34 93 307 6501
www.fortezacarbonell.com

Smith and Thompson Architects
501 West 26th Street, New York,
NY 10011, USA
T: +1 212 924 4358
F: +1 212 924 8917
smithth1@aol.com

tele-design
2-12-5 Mita, Minato-Ku, Tokyo, Japan
T: +81 3 3769 0833
F: +81 3 3769 9893
tele-web@tele-design.net
www.tele-design.net

Tom McCallum, Shania Shegedyn
shaniashegedyn@bigpond.com

Vicens + Ramos
Barquillo 29, 2° izqda., 28004 Madrid, Spain
T: +34 91 521 0004
F: +34 91 521 6550
vicensramos@arquired.es

Wood + Zapata
444 Broadway, 3rd floor, New York,
NY 10013, USA
T: +1 212-966-9292
F: +1 212-966-9242
www.wood-zapata.com

Yasushi Ikeda, Akiko Kokubun / IKDS
3-10-1 Aobadai, Meguroku,
Tokyo, Japan
T: +81 3 3461 3327
www.ik-ds.com

Ziba Khalili
307 East 89th Street Suite 4G, New York,
NY 10128, USA
T: +1 212 860 0112
F: +1 212 831 2859